T0003262

Jane Fonda

In Her Own Words

Jane Fonda

In Her Own Words

EDITED BY
**Amanda Gibson
and Kelsey Dame**

A B2 BOOK

AGATE

CHICAGO

Printed in United States of America

Jane Fonda: In Her Own Words

Cataloging-in-Publication Data is available from the Library of Congress.

ISBN 13: 978-1-57284-302-8
ISBN 10: 1-57284-302-0
eISBN 13: 978-1-57284-861-0
eISBN 10: 1-57284-861-8

First printing: May 2022

10 9 8 7 6 5 4 3 2 1   22 23 24 25 26

B2 Books is an imprint of Agate Publishing. Agate books are available in bulk at discount prices. For more information, go to agatepublishing.com.

Nothing's fun if it's not controversial.

—JANE FONDA

Contents

Introduction...1

Part I: Upbringing

Henry & Frances...6

Forgiveness..13

Part II: Acting

Foundations..18

Success & Purpose...26

The Return..36

Part III: Men & Marriage

Vadim..43

Tom...47

Ted..50

Parenting..54

Just Jane...61

Part IV: Political Activism

Vietnam..70

Social Justice...80

Power of the People..94

Part V: Gender

Expectations...102

Feminism...109

Female Friendship 115

Part VI: Environmentalism

Not a Drill 120

Jail Time 132

Part VII: Health & Well-Being

Body 138

Mind 149

Spirit 156

Milestones 171

Acknowledgments 192

Introduction

JANE FONDA DOESN'T DO THINGS HALFWAY. Whether it's accompanying sex workers to research a film role, visiting Vietnam to gather evidence of a U.S. administration's lies, or leaving stardom behind to fly-fish with a new husband—she's the first to admit that she throws herself into her endeavors "500 percent."

Fonda grew up in the shadow of her parents, acclaimed actor Henry Fonda and socialite Frances Ford Seymour. At their Santa Monica mountain home, Jane spent her days climbing trees, imagining herself as the Lone Ranger—independent and untamed. But her home life was darkened by her parents' mental health struggles.

She had witnessed her mother's toxic striving for physical perfection and wanted little to do with femininity as a result. Then in 1950, when Jane was twelve, her mother died by suicide. Afterward, Jane constantly sought her father's approval, defined by his expectations and mimicking his aversion to intimacy.

Eventually she took an acting class with director and coach Lee Strasberg, who told her she had talent. Jane had found both approval and her passion.

By the early '60s, Jane was a film star. She was living in France when she fell into the orbit of director Roger Vadim, whom she married two years later. Vadim directed Jane in multiple films, including 1968's sci-fi spoof *Barbarella*, which earned Jane her sex symbol status.

Later that year, their child Vanessa was born. Jane experienced postpartum depression and felt she lacked the tools to connect with her daughter. Her marriage suffered as well, as she began to recognize Vadim's alcoholism and gambling addiction, though her desire to remain the ideal '60s housewife rendered her silent and deferential.

But in the late 1960s and early '70s, Jane's film roles were changing, and so was she. She turned toward more serious roles, one of which was *Klute*'s Bree Daniels, a sex worker who gets wrapped up in a murder mystery. Jane spent time with sex workers to research the role, and her performance won the Academy Award for Best Actress.

By then, she and Vadim had separated, and Jane was focusing on something else: the war in Vietnam. After reading a report on the American destruction of a Vietnamese village, Jane felt unable to ignore the devastating impact of the war and flung herself into the anti-war effort. During this time, she met and fell in love with fellow activist Tom Hayden.

In 1972, Jane flew to Vietnam to record evidence that President Nixon had been lying about the de-escalation of the war. She traveled through the countryside, sheltering during bomb raids and filming American-incurred damage. While visiting a military base, she sat down on an anti-aircraft gun. Photographers captured the moment and the image made headlines, casting her as anti-American and leading to the nickname "Hanoi Jane."

Despite the controversy, Jane continued her anti-war efforts with new husband Tom, bringing their infant son Troy along on the road. The couple would also later informally adopt a teenager named Mary Luana Williams ("Lulu"), who attended the performing arts summer camp they'd founded in Santa Barbara.

Through the '70s, Jane continued to make films that were relevant to issues she cared about. One was *Coming*

Home, which addressed the emotional damage of the Vietnam War and earned her a second Academy Award.

Jane and Tom founded the Campaign for Economic Democracy (CED) after the war to promote labor rights and anti-pollution initiatives in California. To help raise funds for CED, she opened a Beverly Hills studio called Workout. It evolved into a 1982 exercise video that would become the best-selling home video of all time and spark a global fitness phenomenon.

The *Workout* series didn't just raise millions of dollars for CED—it brought Jane back into her body, helping her to break out of decades of disembodiment and eating disorders. But Tom saw her exercise empire like he saw her films: as "vanity projects." Eventually he admitted he was in love with someone else, and their marriage ended in 1990.

Almost immediately, media mogul Ted Turner called, eager to court Jane. She had hesitations about diving into another relationship so soon, but Ted was endearing and relentless, and they married in 1991. Ted wanted Jane to focus on him, and she wanted her third marriage to work, so she retired from acting and followed him across the plains from one fly-fishing spot to the next. During this period, she discovered a new calling: philanthropy. She founded the Georgia Campaign for Adolescent Power and Potential (GCAPP) in the mid-90s as a teen pregnancy prevention program.

Approaching sixty, Jane took a long, honest look at her history. Her research and reflection revealed truths about herself, her mother, and her upbringing that allowed her to heal old wounds. It also gave her the courage to leave Ted. In 2001 they divorced, and Jane refocused on the work that she'd started with GCAPP. In

2005 she returned to making films and went on to star on Broadway and television, earning Tony and Emmy nominations. Her role on the Netflix series *Grace and Frankie* introduced a new generation of viewers to Jane's acting and launched her back into the public discourse—just in time for her to return to activism in her whole-hearted way.

After reading about Greta Thunberg's work to elevate climate change issues to the level of societal emergency, Jane was moved, just as she had been after reading about Vietnam. With urgent determination, she launched Fire Drill Fridays in Washington, D.C., marching to the steps of the Capitol each Friday in late 2019, engaging in civil disobedience, and waiting to be arrested. Jane once again committed herself 500 percent.

While she spent decades of her life feeling less than whole, Jane Fonda has never hesitated to fight for the wholeness of others. Her wins and missteps have been in the interest of pushing the needle closer toward a more empathetic and compassionate world. And her words serve as a roadmap for getting there, as well as proof that it's never too late for any of us to evolve.

Part I

UPBRINGING

Henry &

Frances

I WAS HENRY Fonda's daughter, which, of
course, meant that I was polite, I was nice . . .
I was the girl next door. All of the things that I
didn't feel I was. I didn't like my body. I didn't like
myself. I felt shy. We looked like the American
Dream. Rich, beautiful, close, but a lot of it was
simply myth.

—*Jane Fonda in Five Acts*, 2018

I GREW UP in the Santa Monica mountains, and I
knew all the little animals, and the bugs, and the
skunks, and the coyotes, and I loved them. The
household wasn't very happy, so that's where I
found happiness.

—*Jane Fonda in Five Acts*, 2018

IN THE CONFINES of our home, Dad's darker side would emerge. We, his intimates, lived in constant awareness of the minefield we had to tread so as not to trigger his rage. This environment of perpetual tension sent me a message that danger lies in intimacy, that far away is where it is safe.

—*My Life So Far*, 2005

[DAD] WAS A hero to so many people. But these kind of men aren't always good fathers. It's hard to be both.

—*Jane Fonda in Five Acts*, 2018

YOU KNOW, WHEN your father doesn't show up for you or isn't able to really show you that he loves you unconditionally, then you spend a lot of your life trying to be lovable rather than authentic.

—*New York Times*, September 21, 2018

[MOTHER] WAS VERY extroverted but never fought for herself and didn't stand up for what she believed in. Had a tremendous amount of energy and talent that had no outlet. And I know too many women who get burnt up when all the outlets are blocked, they have no way to express themselves and there's no context in which they can do it. And it's very destructive.

—NBC Dallas–Fort Worth, 1980

MY MOTHER KILLED herself when I was 12. She suffered from bipolar disorder, severe. And I didn't really know her that well. And I dedicated the [memoir] to her as a way to force myself to find out who she was.

—*Charlie Rose*, April 17, 2006

WHEN A PARENT is suffering from major depression and when they commit suicide, the child always thinks it's their fault.

—*Charlie Rose*, April 17, 2006

DURING MY CHILDHOOD, I could have gone down a dark hole, but my resilience was like radar constantly scanning the horizon, picking up on heat from anybody who could give me love or teach me something. Resilient people can turn their wounds into swords and ploughshares.

—*Harvard Business Review*, March–April, 2018

EVEN WHEN I found out my mother died, I didn't cry or anything, and people would say, "Isn't she amazing? She's so strong." That became the rap on me.... That got me through. *I'm strong.* But then later on in life, what happens is you become a person who won't express needs, won't express vulnerability, won't turn to anybody for help.

—*I Weigh with Jameela Jamil* podcast, April 23, 2021

MY INTEREST IN what men think about me started with my father. I saw myself in him, and I wanted his approval.

—*W Magazine*, May 19, 2015

I HEARD MY father say things about my body that has twisted my life in deep ways ever since.

—*Jane Fonda in Five Acts*, 2018

MOTHERS ARE OFTEN blamed for that, but for me, it was my dad. I made him ashamed. He thought I was fat, because I didn't look the way he wanted me to look.

—on bulemia, *Jane Fonda in Five Acts*, 2018

MY FATHER'S STAR was the one I wanted to hitch my wagon to. He was the winning team. And whatever it took to make him love me, I would do. And it was hard to feel that he loved you.

—*Charlie Rose*, April 7, 2005

IT WAS HIS generation. It was the fact that he came from the Midwest. You don't express emotion. You don't ask for things. You don't express any kind of need.

—on her father's undiagnosed depression, *Charlie Rose*,
August 16, 2011

I BATTLED DEPRESSION all my life, I had it on both sides of my family. It's always been a problem.

—*Charlie Rose*, August 16, 2011

Forgiveness

MY PARENTS DID the best they could. They were very nice, wonderful, wounded people.

—Charlie Rose, **April 17, 2006**

YOU HAVE TO learn as much as you can about your parents. Learn about them as people: Why was this person the way he was? After that you will realize that their treatment of you—as a child, as an adult—had nothing to do with you. If they had a problem loving you, it was because they didn't know how.

—Town & Country, **October 12, 2017**

I GOT [MOTHER'S] medical records. . . . And in it I discovered that she had been sexually abused. And the minute I knew that . . . I wanted so to be able to hold her and tell her that I understood everything and I forgave her.

—Larry King Live, **April 6, 2005**

THAT SHADOW OF guilt and hatred of body can be passed on to daughters. And I certainly inherited it. And I didn't know that the shadow that I was living under for so long was the shadow of my mother's [experiences of] abuse.

—*Charlie Rose*, **April 17, 2006**

I CAN NOW understand that my mother was all the things that people have described—the icon, the flame, the follow-spot—and also all that I had felt as a child—a victim, a beautiful but damaged butterfly, unable to give me what I needed—to be loved, seen—because she could not give it to herself.

—*My Life So Far*, **2005**

I MISS [DAD] so much, I think I'd be able to talk to him now, which was something I had a hard time doing when he was alive; I was too intimidated by him. There's so much that I wasn't able to say.

—*Town & Country*, **October 12, 2017**

I UNDERSTAND [DAD]. And I worked hard to
understand him. And I've forgiven him. He did
the best he could. There's a lot of fathers like
that.

—*Larry King Live*, April 6, 2005

IF YOU DIDN'T know where I came from—
emotionally, psychically and all kinds of ways—
then where I've ended up doesn't really make
that much difference.

—on telling the truth in her memoir, *New York Times*,
April 5, 2005

IT'S NOT WHAT was done to you, it's what you do
with it that makes a life. And I worked very hard
to take that early lack of parenting and turn it
into something positive.

—*The Margaret Throsby Interviews*, 2006

Part II

ACTING

Foundations

WHEN I WAS young, I didn't want to be an
actress because my father . . . he never seemed to
bring joy home when he came home from work.

—*Oprah's Master Class*, January 8, 2012

I FELT THAT I wasn't any of the things you
needed to be to be an actor. I was shy. I thought I
was unattractive. I just didn't see myself that way
at all.

—CUNY TV's *Theater Talk*, May 2, 2009

THE CAMERA FELT like my enemy. Standing
before it, I felt as though I were falling off a cliff
with no net under me. There was so much focus
on externals, and there seemed no shortage of
people who let me know that my externals could
use some improvement.

—*My Life So Far*, 2005

WHEN YOU GROW up in the industry, and you see what the people are really like behind their masks, you know, you're not too encouraged to become an actor.

—*Jane Fonda in Five Acts*, 2018

I GOT INTO it by default. I was fired as a secretary. I had to do something to earn a living. And because of *my* father, I got to know Lee Strasberg's daughter, Susan, who encouraged me to study with *her* father, which I didn't really want to do. But, you know, I had to do something.

—*Charlie Rose*, April 17, 2006

THIS AUGUST TEACHER of some of the great actors in America said, "You have talent." And, you know, kind of the top of my head came off and birds flew out and it changed my life.

—on studying under Lee Strasberg, *The Margaret Throsby Interviews*, 2006

IT WAS A theater on Broadway, and [the director] called me down to the footlight and he looked up at me and he said, "Are you ambitious?" And I said, "No. No." The minute the words came out of my mouth I knew I'd lost the part. You know and it was like, why did I say that? I said that because good girls are not ambitious.

—*Charlie Rose*, **August 16, 2011**

I HAVE TO be very honest. I am Henry Fonda's daughter. I have always had privilege. When it was very slow going in terms of my ability to earn a living, I had savings that I could fall back on. I don't want to pretend that I was scraping nickels and dimes together. I lived pretty close to the bone for quite a while, but I always knew I could make it. I have to say that. My privilege protected me a lot.

—*Interview Magazine*, **October 7, 2020**

I REMEMBER ONE terrible, agonizing audition when Tyrone Guthrie said to me, "What else have you ever done besides be Henry Fonda's daughter?" So instead of doing a scene a month in class, I'd do two a week, compensating for being a Fonda by working twice as hard as everybody else. Then if I got a part I could say it was because I worked for it.

—*New York Times*, January 25, 1970

I DID FIVE plays on Broadway when I was just starting out. I did not enjoy them.... It takes so much out of you, eight performances a week.. . that every nook and cranny of your psyche is filled with this. You have to totally not think of or do anything else.

—British Film Institute, November 16, 2018

IN THEATER EVERY night, you either show up or you don't. You're either there 100% or you're not. You get it right away from the audience, and it's like a breathing character in the play.

—CUNY TV's *Theater Talk*, May 2, 2009

I DIDN'T KNOW how to say no. I was offered parts that I never should have said yes to because I was afraid that a second one wouldn't come along.

—Charlie Rose, **August 16, 2011**

I'D MADE ONE movie before, which was *Tall Story*, and it was a terrible experience. And I hated playing the nice girl next door. So I got a chance to play a hooker, and so I really wanted to sink my teeth into it.

—on *Walk on the Wild Side*, British Film Institute, November 16, 2018

I HAVE A sense of humor now, so I can watch the movie and find it funny. I don't find it sexy, but I find it charming and funny. I don't remember the bad stuff.

—on *Barbarella*, British Film Institute, November 16, 2018

I DID FOUR movies with [Robert Redford]. . . . I was in love with him each time. He was two hours late every day, but I was so gaga that it didn't matter. . . . I made my last movie with him, and I realized I'd finally grown up, because I got really angry when he was two hours late every day.

—**British Film Institute, November 16, 2018**

I HARDLY EVEN read a scene before I do it. I get good ideas when I do it without preconception. You just have to relax, to be clear and open to inspiration. The beauty of movies is that if it's not right—you just do it over again. You just gotta be open to things and you gotta be brave.

—***Rolling Stone*, March 9, 1978**

IT'S A CAREER that's very good for the heart and very bad for the nerves.

—**SAG-AFTRA Foundation, June 24, 2016**

I THINK MOST actors are pretty innocent. . . .
There's an innocence about people whose art is
channeled through their body and their energy
field, and the heart has to be kept open. It's hard
to be a good actor if you're cynical.

—SAG-AFTRA Foundation, June 24, 2016

IT'S ONE OF the reasons that I'm in therapy
again, is to try to understand the relationship
between the actor and his or her wounds, and the
characters that we have to play, because we have
to somehow find the wounds in the character
that are parallel to our own, and we have to have
empathy. It's very difficult to act a character that
you don't have empathy for.

—*BUILD Series*, April 9, 2015

I DO GO back, just to sort of learn what I've
learned. I'm not always sure I've learned
anything, so I like to go back to see if, in fact, I
have.

—on whether she rewatches her old films, SAG-AFTRA
Foundation, June 24, 2016

Success &

Purpose

EVERYTHING WAS A surprise to me. I was
surprised that I got cast in a movie. I was
surprised that I was ever accepted as a model at
Eileen Ford's agency and surprised that I ever
ended up on the cover of *Vogue*. So my life has
just been one big surprise for me.

—*Vogue*, July 9, 2019

I BECAME AN actress because I needed love
and support from a lot of people, but I never
dreamed I'd end up in the movies. It's a troubling
profession because it puffs up your ego, then
kicks it down, and you have to learn to base your
needs on something other than mass love.

—*New York Times*, January 25, 1970

YOU HAVE TO learn how to get down off the
screen and be a real person again. If you start
believing the screen, then one day you wake up
and you are nothing inside, just another pretty
face that isn't so pretty any more.

—*New York Times*, January 25, 1970

I'VE ALWAYS FELT vulnerable when I went out to promote one of my movies. And everytime I've said that to the press at one of these group interviews, I've felt like a bleeding person in a river full of piranhas. I can sense their surprise— she bleeds.

—*Chicago Tribune*, December 29, 1986

I SPENT A week, before we started shooting, in New York with call girls and madams. . . . And I would spend all day with them. I would go with—when they would get their cocaine, and cut their cocaine, and after-hours clubs with their Johns—and the entire time, not one man made a move on me, didn't even wink. . . . I mean, why? What's the matter with me? And I realized that I really wasn't right for the part, that they could see through me.

—on preparing for *Klute*, British Film Institute, November 16, 2018

I REMEMBERED THAT I had known some very, very high-class call girls in France, and what had interested me about them was that they could have been any number of other things. They weren't just beautiful; they were intelligent enough to have led other kinds of lives. Most of them had been sexually abused. . . . That kind of led me in, and Alan [Pakula] and I did a lot of work around all the psychological things that sexual abuse does to a female.

—**American Film Institute, March 9, 2021**

KLUTE WAS A turning point in my life and in my career. *Coming Home* was too, because it was the first movie that I was involved in the production and it spoke to things that mattered a lot to me.

—*Charlie Rose*, **April 17, 2006**

WINNING THE ACADEMY Award [for *Klute*] was
a huge event for me as an actress; whatever else
happened, I would always have that. But nothing
really changed in my life—not that I expected
it to. Yet there's always a vague hope that such
acclaim will make everything else fall into place.
It doesn't.

—*My Life So Far*, 2005

YOU KNOW THE two times that I won an Oscar, I
did my own hair and makeup. When I picked up
the Oscar for my dad, it looked like the Lindbergh
baby was hidden in my hair . . . I mean, it was the
'80s, just to be fair to myself.

—*Jane Fonda in Five Acts*, 2018

I HAD NEVER made a movie that was *about*
something, that came out at the right time and
had something to say about capitalism, about
greed, about the things that were wrong with
American society.

—on *They Shoot Horses, Don't They?*, British Film
Institute, November 16, 2018

ONE NIGHT I went to see Lily [Tomlin] in her one-woman show, *Appearing Nitely,* and what can I say, I was smitten, and I said, I don't want to make a movie about secretaries unless she's in it.

—on producing *9 to 5,* *The Late Show with Stephen Colbert,* March 28, 2017

IT TOOK ME almost a year to convince [Lily] to be in *9 to 5.* And after filming one week, she talked to my co-producer, Bruce Gilbert, and said, "Let me go. Let me out of my contract." . . . Even when you have the genius of Lily Tomlin, you still can be filled with, you know, questioning and self-doubt.

—SAG-AFTRA Foundation, June 24, 2016

THE QUESTION IS simply, "When wealthy or famous people become part of a movement that speaks primarily to the interest of the poor and the middle class, what do you do with the unecessary profit?" Once I resolved that confict, I saw no reason to give up acting.

—*Washington Post,* October 28, 1977

DURING HISTORIC TRANSITIONS, art has always been critical. It reminds us that the world as it is, is not all there is, that there are other possibilities to strive for.

—*Jane Fonda* blog, April 20, 2020

I GUESS THE main criterion that I have for choosing roles is, "Do they tell the truth?" You can tell the truth with a song, with a laugh, with a tragedy, in a lot of different ways. But I'd rather not work than make any more movies that lie.

—BBC's *Tonight*, 1976

IF YOU WANT to do a movie that's *about* something, you have to decide what's the style that it needs to be dressed in. For example, the very first movie that was kind of my idea was *Coming Home*. That was a sexy love story. So that even if you didn't care about the well-being of Vietnam veterans, you could like the movie because it was sexy.

—*Keep It!* podcast, March 25, 2020

My acting improved when I became an activist—I see things from a broader perspective.

—*Porter* magazine, March 2, 2017

IN TURBULENT, CRISIS-TORN times like these, storytelling has always been essential. You see, stories . . . they can change our hearts and our minds. They can help us see each other in a new light, to have empathy, to recognize that for all our diversity, we are humans first, right?

—**Golden Globe Awards, February 28, 2021**

CAN YOU IMAGINE, what a gift for a daughter who has had a difficult relationship with her father to find a property like that, this play, and to be able to produce it for him in a role that has so paralleled what happened in real life, and then to have him win an Oscar for it. I'm a very lucky person.

—**on making *On Golden Pond* with her father, *Charlie Rose*, August 16, 2011**

IF YOU HIT a place in life, which a lot of women do in their late 40s—it's called perimenopause, where you get really down on yourself, and you really get depressed and you see no future—I found it very hard to be creative. Acting became agony. And I just thought, "I can't do it, it's just too painful." So I left.

—on why she left acting, SAG-AFTRA Foundation,
June 24, 2016

The Return

BY THE TIME I finished writing my memoir, I was a different person, and I thought, "I can find joy in acting again," and then this script came along. And I've never thought strategically about my career in my life, but I thought . . . my part is the better part. People are going to come to see Jennifer Lopez, but they're going to find Jane Fonda, or *re-find* Jane Fonda.

—on deciding to return to acting in *Monster-in-Law*,
British Film Institute, November 16, 2018

IT'S SO RARE to find a multi-dimensional part for women, older women in particular, and when they come along you grab them. . . . So my process is, you follow the good writing.

—on selecting roles for herself, *BUILD Series*,
April 9, 2015

IT'S LIKE SEX and riding a bike; it comes back.

—on returning to acting, *Happy Sad Confused* podcast,
January 16, 2018

PART TWO *The Return*

I WAS ONE of those movie people who, for a long time, was snobbish about TV. . . . I'm old. Television is more forgiving for older women, and so I said, "Okay, I'm going to start paying attention." So I started watching TV, and now I don't know if I'm going to go back into movie theaters. I just love television.

—*Harper's BAZAAR*, **March 25, 2021**

COMEDY IS MUCH harder than drama, and there's a certain rhythm. Lily [Tomlin] knows that in her DNA and I don't.

—*Happy Sad Confused* **podcast, January 16, 2018**

I DON'T FEEL funny. I guess I shouldn't say that, but I come from a long line of depressed people.

—*Keep It!* **podcast, March 25, 2020**

38 **JANE FONDA** IN HER OWN WORDS

I THINK ONE of the reasons the show is so
popular is that, oh god, in this day and age, we
need something that doesn't cause anxiety.

—on *Grace and Frankie*, *BUILD Series*, **January 15, 2018**

WE PLAY OLDER women who are not going down
easy, and we have a lot of piss and vinegar and
vibrators and things like that, and sex.

—on *Grace and Frankie*, *BUILD Series*, **January 15, 2018**

THE MORE WE can get issues like aging, and the
issues of sexual identity, and so forth into the
zeitgeist, the better it is. Television happens to be
a really good medium for older people.

—on the influence of *Grace and Frankie*, **SAG-AFTRA
Foundation, June 24, 2016**

BECAUSE OF GLOBALIZATION, the major studios, to make a lot of money, have to do movies that will appeal in China, and India, and France, and all over the world, and that usually means that a certain kind of man has to be in the lead, and there has to be a lot of action, and a lot of special effects because that plays across cultures. Character-driven stories and comedies don't necessarily play across cultures. . . . And that kind of leaves out old women . . . so we have to kind of scrounge around and get funding for independent films.

—**British Film Institute, November 16, 2018**

WHEN I STARTED back in '59, the only women you ever saw on a set were the script supervisors, and there were no other women anywhere. And now we have focus pullers and gaffers and there's women all over the place.

—**SAG-AFTRA Foundation, June 24, 2016**

I'M NOT A good leader. I look like a leader, but I'm not. I'm very uncomfortable being out front. What I love about movie-making or television is the collaborative part of it, people working together. I never liked to be the head. I freeze.

—on why she chooses not to direct, *Harper's BAZAAR*, **March 25, 2021**

ACTING HAS NEVER been what's healed me. Activism has, but not acting.

—*Washington Post*, **September 20, 2018**

Part III

MEN & MARRIAGE

Vadim

I COULD WRITE one version of my marriage to Vadim in which he would come across as a cruel, misogynistic, irresponsible wastrel. I could also write him as the most charming, lyrical, poetic, tender of men. Both versions would be true.

—*My Life So Far*, 2005

FRANKLY, IF I had it all to do over, knowing then what I know now, I would have plunged in just the same.

—on marrying Vadim, *My Life So Far*, 2005

VADIM WAS SO full of contradictions. There were a lot of issues that I just chose not to see. I didn't know what compulsive gambling was, or alcoholism. If I would complain, he would call me bourgeois.

—*Jane Fonda in Five Acts*, 2018

I WAS SO conditioned to identify with men
in every possible way. When I was married to
Roger Vadim, one day one of his friends said,
"God, Jane, you're just like us"—and I took it as a
compliment!

—Vogue UK, April 3, 2019

I JUST NEVER thought that I was good enough.
And I was prepared to betray myself, my body
and my heart, in order to keep him. And I thought
long and hard about whether or not to write
about it in the book. I could have just said, "All
through my life I have betrayed myself in order
to please the man I was with," and left it at that,
kind of theoretical. But I decided to put some
flesh on that. And I thought it was important to
show how deep misogyny goes.

—on saying "yes" to Vadim's request to bring other
women into their bed, Charlie Rose, April 17, 2006

I KNEW THAT if I threw myself heart and
soul into the anti-war effort, a return to the
permissive, indolent life I shared with Vadim
would be unthinkable.

—*My Life So Far*, 2005

I WAS GONNA have to leave Vadim, and that
whole hedonistic relationship. And I think it was
deeply confusing for him to have a wife that he
cared for leave him, not for another man, but for
an idea.

—*Jane Fonda in Five Acts*, 2018

Tom

FOR ME [TOM] was the white knight who had arrived in my life just in the nick of time to set everything straight and save me from chaos. Poor Tom. How unfair projections are. No mortal man could possibly live up to that.

—*My Life So Far*, 2005

WE DELIVERED OUR message—demand that Congress cut aid to our puppet regime in Saigon—in union halls, churches, editorial boards, on campuses, to crowds of sometimes 10,000 people. We distributed over a million pieces of educational literature. I got pregnant during the tour in a motor home en route to Buffalo, NY. That was part of our shared commitment to the future.

—*Jane Fonda* blog, March 2, 2017

I NEEDED SOMEONE far wiser and more knowledgeable than I was about movement-building and politics and all of that. And he had this depth of knowledge, and he gave me structure and guidance, and I learned so much from him that I am forever grateful for.

—*New Yorker*, September 26, 2018

I STARTED GETTING more work, winning a second Oscar with *Coming Home*, started The Workout—to fund the organization we started—but still [Tom] hated it, because he saw it as a vanity project. And we just grew apart.

—PeopleTV, September 20, 2018

[TOM] FELL IN love with somebody, and I found out. It did knock the foundation out from under me because I just never could have imagined life without Tom. If I'm not with Tom Hayden, then I'm nobody.

—*Jane Fonda in Five Acts*, 2018

Ted

THE DAY AFTER my divorce from Tom Hayden was announced, the phone rang, and this booming Southern accent, he said, "Would you want to go out with me?" And I said, "Well, I'm having a nervous breakdown. Call me in six months." And six months to the day, Ted asked me out again.

—Jane Fonda in Five Acts, 2018

IN HIS HEART, Ted is not a wealthy, powerful, privileged person. He's a little boy who likes to play, and who has wild brilliance, and that's what I was attracted to.

—Jane Fonda in Five Acts, 2018

WE WERE BOTH children of suicide, so we understood each other.

—Jane Fonda in Five Acts, 2018

YOU KNOW WHEN I really realized that I'm in love with this man? We were at his place in Montana . . . and he leaned out of the window and he said, "That's a peregrine falcon." . . . It was just the silhouette. I said, "He knows birds by their silhouette and how they fly?" He taught me about wildlife. He taught me about nature. He taught me about how to manage land; how to be a good steward of the land. He taught me about exploring and adventure. Oh, he taught me a lot.

—*Charlie Rose*, August 16, 2011

TED TURNER IS seriously funny, so a lot of the stuff he used to say, I've stolen. So, I can fool people into thinking I'm funny. I owe him a great debt of gratitude.

—*Keep It!* podcast, March 25, 2020

I KNEW I would die married, rich, but not whole.

—on her decision to leave Ted, *Oprah's Master Class: The Podcast*, September 19, 2018

TED AND I had a really, really good time. . . . But he likes to move all the time, from one of his houses to another to another. He lives laterally, and I wanted to live vertically: I wanted to stay put, and he always wanted to go.

—*W Magazine*, May 19, 2015

[TED] ALWAYS WANTED to keep moving and keep moving. I feel like I was evolving. I was growing, and it was hard on him. He couldn't slow down, and so I left.

—*Conversations* podcast, September 11, 2020

WHEN HE AND I split up, he said, "But you're not supposed to change after sixty." And I said, "Well, I think it's dangerous not to." And I'm glad that I continued to change and grow and evolve. That's what separates us from other animals.

—*Charlie Rose*, April 17, 2006

Parenting

I KNEW THAT I was pregnant and I remember
going to my car and sitting and just terrified
because this was absolute proof that I was
a woman and that meant I was going to be
destroyed.

—SiriusXM, September 25, 2018

MY CHILDHOOD DIDN'T teach me how to be a
very good parent.

—*Your Teen* magazine, 2014

I BECAME AN activist shortly after [Vanessa] was
born, and I was off. I was on the barricades. . . .
And I didn't bring her with me. I should have.

—SiriusXM, September 25, 2018

MARRIED TO VADIM, we had a governess. And
Tom wouldn't put up with it. And so we took Troy
everywhere with us. And I was a little bit more
mature then.

—*Charlie Rose*, April 17, 2006

I'VE STUDIED PARENTING . . . and I came to understand what good parenting looks like. I didn't know that when I became a parent so I just . . . didn't know what to do.

—*All Things Considered*, September 24, 2018

I WISH I'D done more talking. I wasn't consistent enough. And I traveled a lot. I hate to think it, but I sort of repeated some of my parents' mistakes.

—on parenting regrets, *Your Teen* magazine, 2014

I DIDN'T KNOW how to be an approachable and askable parent, starting quite early. I didn't know how to listen and not be judgmental.

—*Charlie Rose*, March 11, 2014

I NEEDED TO forgive my mother and to love myself more before I would learn how to be a better mother to Vanessa.

—*My Life So Far*, 2005

IF I HAD it to do over, I would have seen her for the beautiful being that she is. I would have taken her with me, the way I did later with my son. . . . I would have been present.

—on daughter Vanessa, *Charlie Rose*, April 7, 2005

I PARTICIPATED IN taking the voice of my daughter away. I can look at photographs of her now, before early adolescence and after adolescence, and I can see what I did to her, without realizing what I was doing.

—*O, The Oprah Magazine*, July 2000

SHE HAS BEEN angry with me most of her life. . . . And we have had a very prickly, problematic relationship, because when she was little, I really never showed up. I did what my parents did to me.

—on her relationship with Vanessa, *Charlie Rose*, April 17, 2006

INTUITIVELY, VANESSA HAS always known my strength—and she has always seen me give it up for a man. It has made her very angry.

—O, The Oprah Magazine, July 2000

MY DAUGHTER IS a fantastic mother in spite of my weaknesses as a parent. . . . Her second child is a daughter and she said, "I'm going to show that mothers and daughters can be really, really close," and she succeeded.

—Charlie Rose, August 16, 2011

WHEN I WATCH my son and his wife, Simone, parent, I'm awestruck. It puts into such stark relief for me, what I didn't do. . . . Watching my son be a parent, I think, "God, I just wish I had done that." And then I realize, if I had done that I would not have become who I became.

—Harper's BAZAAR, March 25, 2021

THERE'S THIS MIRACLE that happens in life. When your children become adults and then you have to make this switch and realize that you can learn from them. It's beautiful.

—*Larry King Live*, **April 6, 2005**

YOU DON'T WANT to get to the end saying, "Well, God, I got all the awards and I got all the money and I did all that, but my kids don't like me." I don't want that.

—*Charlie Rose*, **April 7, 2005**

CHILDREN GO AWRY when their parents demand them to live up to their expectations. It's a fantastic liberation when the parents learn how to let go.

—*New York Times*, **January 25, 1970**

IF YOU INSTILL that unconditional love in your children, they're not going to feel that they need to be perfect in order to be loved.

—Charlie Rose, **April 17, 2006**

IT'S NEVER TOO late to be a parent. It's never too late to let the child know. My not being there for you had nothing to do with you. It was my issue, not you.

—Charlie Rose, **April 17, 2006**

I'M NOW FIVE years older than my dad was when he died and I've realized that I am, in fact, stronger than he was. I'm stronger than all the men that I've been married to.

—The Guardian, **September 5, 2020**

BOY, I SHOULD win Oscars for how I can become whatever the man wants me to be, and I went through three marriages like that.

—4D with Demi Lovato **podcast, June 16, 2021**

Just Jane

MY DAD WAS married five times. I wasn't dealt a good hand of cards in terms of relationships. I'm not gifted at relationships.

—*The Times*, **September 8, 2020**

I WAS CERTAIN that in each case of my three husbands that I was moving towards a man who was the polar opposite of my father. Uh-uh. Superficially, but deep down . . . they were not able to show up.

—**PeopleTV, September 27, 2018**

IF A GUY had come along and said, "Come on, Fonda, show up," I would have run away scared. I was attracted to men who never would have done that to me because they couldn't necessarily show up themselves.

—*Harper's BAZAAR*, **March 25, 2021**

I MEAN, MEN want to get married. I had two
important relationships subsequent to Ted, they
wanted to get married. They were obsessed with
it, because it's possession.

—*Chicago Tribune*, **September 22, 2018**

NONE OF MY marriages were democratic,
because I was too worried about pleasing. I had
to be a certain way in order for them to love me.
I had to look a certain way, and I looked different
for all of them. I wanted to be living as a whole
Jane, fully realized Jane.

—*Jane Fonda in Five Acts*, **2018**

WHEN YOU RESIDE within your own skin,
you can feel it. You're holding all of you: your
anger, your kindness, your judgementalness.
Everything that makes up what you are,
including the fact that you may be stronger and
braver than the man you're married to.

—*Jane Fonda in Five Acts*, **2018**

IF I'M IN a relationship that I'm going to regret staying in, that gives me the courage to leave.

—*I Weigh with Jameela Jamil* podcast, April 23, 2021

I HAD REALIZED that I was in a real quandary in terms of human relationships, because most of the men that I had been with were real resentful and overpowered by who I was. Either resentful of my earning capacities, or that I was stifling them or overpowering them. I was denying my own abilities in order not to make them feel bad.

—*Rolling Stone*, March 9, 1978

WHAT I'VE LEARNED is that you can't have a real relationship until you've had one with yourself. You can't really have an intimate relationship until you bring your whole self to the table.

—*Charlie Rose*, April 17, 2006

I HAD BEEN separated from my favorite ex-husband for three days. . . . And I was standing alone in the home of my first-born, who was not there, and although I was very sad, I realized, I'm not scared. This is the first time in my life that I'm without a man, and I'm not scared. And I realized I was becoming whole.

—*BUILD Series*, **April 9, 2015**

I DON'T NEED to be validated by a man. I want someone with no hidden agenda. Someone who can be a real companion and I can have fun with.

—*Charlie Rose*, **August 16, 2011**

I HAVE ALWAYS liked to climb mountains and be alone. But it's more fulfilling to do it when you know that on the other side of the mountain is real relationship.

—*Charlie Rose*, **August 16, 2011**

IT'S LIKE, I deserve respect. I do, and I deserve to be loved. And if somebody can't quite do that, then I'm sorry, I'm not going to hang around.

—*Washington Post*, September 20, 2018

I DO NOT regret those three marriages. They were utterly fascinating men, and I learned a huge amount from all of them.

—*WTF with Marc Maron* podcast, March 28, 2021

I LOVE MEN, I'm not done with men, but I'm done with marriage and dating.

—*The Guardian*, May 27, 2018

YOU KNOW, JUST about every day, I'll be in the middle of something and think, I would never have had time to do this or read this if I was trying to keep a relationship good.

—*New York Times*, September 2, 2020

I AM FULLY complete with me and my children and my grandchildren and my friends. I don't want any more romance.

—*New York Times*, **September 2, 2020**

I DON'T WANT to give myself over. I lose myself. I'm a colander when I'm in a relationship—a full, sexual relationship with a man.

—*WTF with Marc Maron* **podcast, March 28, 2021**

GIVEN MY PARENTS' difficulties with relationships, and my personal evolution, choosing right for the long haul just hasn't been in the cards. I comfort myself in knowing that should I choose again, the haul will be shorter.

—*My Life So Far*, **2005**

I THINK THAT I've overcome the disease to please. But I can't really know, living with a dog.

—*Charlie Rose*, **April 17, 2006**

I'VE WORKED HARD on forgiveness, and that
includes for my three husbands.

—*The Cut*, September 4, 2018

I JUST SORT of know instinctively that when the
end comes ... I'm gonna want to know that I kept
us all together.

—on remaining friends with her ex-husbands and their
families, *WTF with Marc Maron* podcast, March 28,
2021

IN SPITE OF everything, I feel that I chose well.
I learned and grew with Vadim, Tom, and Ted
(sometimes because of them, sometimes in spite
of them), and I feel grateful for that. I also have
to say that in hindsight, each divorce, painful
though it may have been at the time, marked a
step forward, an opportunity for self-redefinition
rather than a failure—almost like repotting a
plant when the roots don't fit anymore.

—*My Life So Far*, 2005

Part IV

POLITICAL ACTIVISM

Vietnam

I READ A book; it was called *The Village of Ben Suc*. It was a small book, and when I finished reading it, my life changed. . . . That was the beginning of my life as an activist, and everything changed because I found meaning in my life.

—*4D with Demi Lovato* podcast, June 16, 2021

BOOKS HAVE ALWAYS been my catalyst.

—interview with @kaiagerber on Instagram, September 30, 2021

I WAS SOMEBODY that really thought that if our soldiers were fighting someplace, we were on the side of the angels. It couldn't be wrong.

—interview with @kaiagerber on Instagram, September 30, 2021

I THOUGHT, OH my God, I feel betrayed by my country, these soldiers have been betrayed by their country. I want to go back and join the movement that's trying to end the war. . . . I left my family, I left my husband, I moved back [to the U.S.] and I never looked back.

—*Bust Magazine*, Winter 2021

MY INTEREST IN the war began because of soldiers and was deepened because of soldiers. It was because of what soldiers told me that I turned against the war.

—*Los Angeles Times*, January 25, 1987

I HAD A child, I was in a marriage. But I felt lost and empty. And when these soldiers opened my mind . . . I was like dry brush and they were this match and, whoosh.

—*Chicago Tribune*, September 22, 2018

I'M A PRODUCT of my times—I'm a kid of the '50s. And in those days no one ever expressed themselves. And I would have gone on that way all my life if it hadn't been for the issue of the war, which just got me in the gut.

—NBC Dallas–Fort Worth, 1980

EVERYONE SEEMS TO think that the word revolution means violence. . . . I mean, any healthy country, like any healthy individual, should be in perpetual revolution, perpetual change.

—CBC Archives, 1970

THIS IS JANE Fonda in Hanoi. I'm speaking to the men in the cockpits of the Phantoms, in the B-52's. . . . If they told you the truth, you wouldn't fight, you wouldn't kill. You were not born and brought up by your mothers to be killers. So you have been told lies so that it would be possible for you to kill.

—Radio Hanoi, July 1972

SOME DAY WE'RE going to have to answer to our children for this war. Some day we are going to have to explain to the rest of the world how it is that we caused this type of suffering and death and destruction to a people who have done us no harm. Perhaps we should start to do it now before it is too late.

—**Radio Hanoi, July 1972**

I BELIEVE THAT in this age of remote-controlled push-button war, we must all try very, very hard to remain human beings.

—**Radio Hanoi, July 1972**

I SAT ON an anti-aircraft gun in North Vietnam. I wasn't even thinking what I was doing. And photographs were taken. And that image went out. And that image makes it look like I was against our soldiers. Which was never the case. I had been working with soldiers prior to that and for years after that.

—***The Tonight Show***, **September 20, 2018**

TO MEN WHO were in Vietnam who I hurt, or whose pain I caused to deepen because of things that I said or did, I feel that I owe them an apology. My intentions were never to hurt them or make their situation worse. It was the contrary. I was trying to help end the killing, end the war. But there were times when I was thoughtless and careless about it.

—20/20, **1988**

[NIXON] WAS BOMBING the dikes and he was lying about it, and I went there to try to expose it. And I'm glad I did.

—Charlie Rose, **April 7, 2005**

HOW MANY MEN died because our presidents were afraid of looking weak? . . . Even now, those who still don't understand, it's sad because I became a lightning rod and I understand why that happened. You have to get mad at somebody, and they can't get mad at the government. So I'm the one.

—British Film Institute, November 16, 2018

THE FAMOUS PHOTOGRAPH of me on an anti-aircraft gun wasn't considered newsworthy until six months after the fact, when President Nixon decided it should be.

—National Press Club, April 14, 2005

IN SOME WAYS we created a silk purse out of a sow's ear. Out of that incident came a lot of communicating, a lot of dialogue about the war and what it meant and what I meant and what I was doing and why I was there.

—regarding the anti-aircraft gun photo, *Charlie Rose*, August 16, 2011

I KNEW WHAT was in my heart. I knew who I was. I knew that I wasn't a traitor and that I didn't intend to do anything that was against the soldiers . . . and so you just go on. And frankly, the more [the FBI] very obviously tried to scare me . . . I'd come home and all the drawers in our house would be torn out . . . the more I just would dig my heels in.

—British Film Institute, November 16, 2018

IF YOU'RE WORRYING people who are doing bad things, then you know you're doing the right thing, I guess.

—*Keep It!* podcast, March 25, 2020

I WAS AWARE that I was being followed, and there was very little attempt to disguise it. There would be these guys in trench coats with dark glasses. The FBI would follow Vanessa to school. The more I saw them, the more my attitude was, "You think I'm gonna back down?"

—*Jane Fonda in Five Acts*, 2018

THE ARRESTING OFFICER told me as he was holding me in his office that he was arresting me under orders from the White House—that would be Richard Nixon.

—WhoWhatWear, January 7, 2020

THE RIGHT WING has been very assiduous in fanning the flame of the myth of Hanoi Jane. You know, they've spread lies on the Internet about things that I supposedly did that aren't true. And they've kept it alive, because it suits their interests.

—*Charlie Rose*, April 17, 2006

I WASN'T BLACKLISTED, but kind of gray-ish listed.

—on her status in Hollywood during the Vietnam War, PeopleTV, September 27, 2018

I NEVER DID let it stop me. I apologize. I try to explain the context. And then I move on.

—on the Hanoi Jane controversy, *New York Times*, September 2, 2020

IT CHANGED ME profoundly, that trip [to Vietnam]. . . . I'm grateful that I went because it taught me so much about what really is strength. You know we're supposedly this big superpower, but we couldn't win. . . . I'm eighty years old and half of my joints are replaced, I won't live that much longer. But I'm really strong now. When I was at the height of my career, I wasn't. It's just a different way of looking at what is strength.

—PeopleTV, September 20, 2018

I'M GRATEFUL TO the FBI because when I was writing my memoirs, I forgot a lot of stuff. . . . 22,000 pages and I never broke the law.

—on the file the FBI kept on her, ACLU SoCal, December 6, 2017

Social

Justice

I'VE STILL GOT a lot of fight left in me.

—*New York Times*, **December 5, 2019**

I SAID TO myself, I don't want to be one of those people who lives on the top of the hill and hands out money to the people who live down in the valley to try to help them. I want to be down in that valley, standing shoulder to shoulder in kinship with those people, and that's what I did.

—*4D with Demi Lovato* **podcast, June 16, 2021**

ACTIVISM BRINGS YOU back into your body. I did not expect or plan on being active like this into my 80s, you know? But it's all I care about.

—*The Cut*, **September 4, 2018**

PEOPLE THINK ACTIVISM is like, "Eat your broccoli." No, it's fun!

—**interview with @kaiagerber on Instagram, September 30, 2021**

ACTIVISM IS THE antidote to despair. Better than Prozac, better than all the other things.

—**National Press Club, December 17, 2019**

THERE'S NOTHING LIKE committing yourself heart, soul, body and mind, to something beyond yourself, that you're willing to die for.

—*The Guardian*, **April 04, 2005**

I'M JUST GLAD the lighting was good!

—**on her infamous 1970 mugshot,** *The Guardian*,
September 5, 2020

WHEN SOMEONE FAMOUS takes a stand, people notice. We get very attacked and that's because it's effective.

—*Bazaar UK*, **November 12, 2020**

CELEBRITY CAN BE really alienating. It separates you from people. It can make you feel lonely, it can make you feel that the people around you are ... they're imposing their own view of who you are and they're not really seeing you for who you are, and so you feel very lonely. And for me, why have celebrity then unless it's gonna be used for something good?

—*BUILD Series*, April 9, 2015

WOMEN WERE VERY much a part of the anti-war movement, but our leadership and intelligence, those parts of us weren't really tapped. In fact, they were shunted aside very often.

—on her early social justice presence during the Vietnam War, *Full Release with Samantha Bee* podcast, September 21, 2020

I STARTED GETTING these emails that had flyers about self-care, why it's important for activists to take care of their health and their mental health, and . . . I've never gotten that from any movement, and then I thought, this must be run by women.

—on the Black Lives Matter movement, interview with @kaiagerber on Instagram, September 30, 2021

HISTORY HAS SHOWN over and over again that whenever we try to solve problems without addressing the issues of inequality and injustice, it never works.

—National Press Club, December 17, 2019

PEOPLE INSIDE THE halls of Congress have to feel pressure from outside. Nothing important has ever happened without it.

—*Jane Fonda* blog, December 17, 2019

DEMOCRACY ISN'T A spectator sport.

—PeopleTV, September 20, 2018

I HAVE NEVER felt the anxiety that I feel right now.... I just turned eighty, I thought I could relax ... maybe study novel writing or gardening or something, and it's back to the barricades.

> —on the current political climate, *BUILD Series*,
> **January 15, 2018**

NOW IS THE time to move from #MeToo to #NeverAgain

> —*The Nation*, **December 13, 2017**

I'M PART OF Time's Up, and I've been to the meetings, and I can tell you, these are not some bubble-headed actresses. These are fierce warriors who understand what it means to be intersectional, to reach out to women of color, to men, to people across sectors.

> —*BUILD Series*, **January 15, 2018**

WHEN POWER AND salaries are equal, women are less vulnerable and men are forced to behave.

—*The Nation*, December 13, 2017

WE'VE SEEN A new concentration of media ownership. Heck, I've been married to it, I saw it happening in my very own bed! The erosion and elimination of federal regulations that promoted a diversity of viewpoints—this has weakened our country, morally, physically, and spiritually.

—National Conference for Media Reform, February 21, 2009

EVERYTHING IS A commodity, so our values have been skewed. What needs to happen is the opposite of capitalism.

—*Interview Magazine*, October 7, 2020

A MEDIA THAT scrambles to tell "both sides" of the story, often leaves out women's side of the story. . . . It's an odd irony that a media establishment that prides itself on balance, forgets that the world is not only divided between right and left, liberals and conservatives, red states and blue. It's also divded by race and by gender. It's divided between women and men. And there's more than two sides to every story.

—National Conference for Media Reform, February 21, 2009

WHEN YOU GO into a dark movie theater and look at a huge LED screen but you're missing from that screen—you never see yourself, your story, your concerns, your beliefs—you feel diminished, you become less. So that's why we feel it's important to try to change that.

—on her organization, the Women's Media Center, *Harvard Business Review*, March–April, 2018

TOO OFTEN, WOMEN feel that they can leave the issue of voting matters to their husbands, or feel fatalistic about the possibility of making a difference; and as a result, issues like healthcare, poverty, forced pregnancy, childcare, and violence aren't up front and center, as they should be.

—**National Press Club, April 14, 2005**

ONE PERSON'S FREEDOMS must logically end at the point where they impinge on another's.

—**LA LGBT Center, November 13, 2015**

WHEN YOU'RE FIGHTING against racism and genocide, you're also fighting for yourself.

—***Vogue*, July 9, 2019**

PEACE CAN'T WAIT for all the white people in the U.S. to rid themselves of racism.

—***Jane Fonda* blog, May 31, 2020**

I'M A WHITE woman and this is something that we white women have to know: you can't just be empathic, you have to be very intentional. We have to confront racism. We have to stop this. Not buy into the lies that we're told about how the prison system stops crime. No, it creates crime.

—The Guardian, May 27, 2018

WHITE PEOPLE NEED to dare imagine the realities inhabited by people of color.

—United States of Women Summit, May 2018

I'M WHITE. I'M privileged. I was my father's daughter, and yet going through adolescence was very, very, very painful for me. That is a period of time that has so much effect on what happens later, and so I thought well if it was that hard for me, imagine for disadvantaged kids, kids of color, poor kids.

—CUNY TV's *Theater Talk*, May 2, 2009

HOPE IS THE best contraceptive. If you help a child see a future for themselves, they will be motivated to either not have sex or to use contraceptives responsibly when they do.

—on her foundation, **Georgia Campaign for Adolescent Power & Potential,** *Associated Press*, **November 12, 2020**

AS PROGRESSIVES, ONE of our tactics must be to forge alliances.

—**National Conference for Media Reform, February 21, 2009**

TAKING THE TIME to engage people across movements makes us stronger.

—*What Can I Do? My Path from Climate Despair to Action*, **2020**

I AM OF the belief that evil deeds, which Trump is committing, is the language of the traumatized. And you can hate the deeds. Don't hate the person because he wins if we hate him. Don't even give him that much energy.

—*New York Times*, September 2, 2020

SO MANY MOVEMENTS have made so much progress that the patriarchy . . . is a wounded beast. And there's nothing more dangerous than a wounded beast.

—*BUILD Series*, January 15, 2018

ONE OF THE good things about being an activist is that you come in contact with woke men.

—*New York Times*, September 2, 2020

The best response to 'divide and conquer' is 'unite and build.'

—Jane Fonda blog, July 4, 2019

THERE'S A LOT of resistance going on ... and that's fantastic, but we have to go beyond "no" to the "yes." What is the "yes" that will beckon us forward to a future that we can all share and embrace?

—*LF Show*, January 19, 2018

I'VE BEEN WORKING with really young people. When you meet them, they give the pronouns that they go by. I'm going on 83. Do I really have to say what pronouns I go by, you know? The answer is yes and there's a learning curve.

—*New York Times*, September 2, 2020

WHEN I WAS younger, I thought that creating social change was a sprint. That you just knew what was right and you just ran and you did it. As I got older, I realized no, it's a marathon, so you have to pace yourself. Now, in my dotage, I realize it's a relay. You have to pass it on, and I am so excited and motivated and inspired by the generations coming up.

—*The Laura Flanders Show*, November 2, 2020

Power of the

People

No big transitions in history have ever happened without an organized, angry public demanding them.

—What Can I Do? My Path from Climate Despair to Action, 2020

It's one of the great things about America. People understand that this is a country that was founded on the principle of freedom of speech, freedom of action, that we have to fight for the right. That's why men and women risk their lives, to defend the notion that we have the right to speak our minds. This is not true in all countries.

—Charlie Rose, April 17, 2006

No country can be strong and healthy if we all don't look out for each other. Maybe rugged individualism worked when this land was a frontier but that's long passed.

—Jane Fonda blog, May 25, 2020

That's what celebrities are. We're repeaters. We don't originate the voice, we pick up the voice and make sure that it reaches a wide audience.

—*Bazaar UK*, November 12, 2020

INDIVIDUALISM WORKS TO the advantage of the relatively few who wield power, and that's why we need to set aside our differences, unify around our common needs, because together is how we gain power.

—*What Can I Do? My Path from Climate Despair to Action*, 2020

WHEN YOU BEGIN to grow a movement, you have to be non-violent. That's when people will join you.

—**interview with @kaiagerber on Instagram, September 30, 2021**

WHEN WE CAN talk to each other, and hear each other as humans, things turn out ok.

—**British Film Institute, November 16, 2018**

IT'S AVERAGE PEOPLE who do extraordinary things because they've been motivated by something very deep within themselves. If you're lucky enough to meet people like that, you can always think back on them and become inspired.

—*BUILD Series*, April 9, 2015

WHAT WAS CONSIDERED radical in the '60s is becoming common sense in the minds of larger numbers of people.

—BBC's *Tonight*, 1976

FEAR CAN BE so powerful, but what overcomes fear is connection.

—*Washington Post*, August 30, 2019

I'VE SEEN THE power of face-to-face contact since I became an activist five decades ago.

—*Washington Post*, August 30, 2019

I have seen so many
people really, really
change. I'm one
of them. I wasn't
always an activist.
Knowing how a
human being can
change, I have a
lot of hope that we
can change enough
people in time.

—*BUILD Series*, January 15, 2018

EVERYONE HAS THE right to speak up; it doesn't matter what you do. Whenever there's been an important revolution or social upheaval, artists, actors, writers and poets are always the people that can reach into areas that politics can't.

—*Porter* magazine, March 2, 2017

NO MATTER HOW good we think the candidate is that we've elected to office, we have to hold their feet to the fire and force them to be accountable to us.

—Working Families Party, October 2020

ALL WORKING PEOPLE, no matter their race, ethnicity, gender, faith, or sexual orientation or gender identity, need a stake and a say in our society—and they all need to hear that they're part of "We the People."

—*Washington Post*, August 30, 2019

Part V

GENERER

Expectations

A LOT OF other people were defining me, all of them men. I never felt real.

—*Jane Fonda in Five Acts*, 2018

I USED TO think I really wanted to be a boy because that's where the action was, and for a while I looked so androgynous that I'd be asked whether I was a boy or a girl. That was the biggest compliment I could get. Looking back, I think I just wanted to be exempt from what was required of girlness.

—*My Life So Far*, 2005

GIRLS LOSE THEIR original spirit in early adolescence. The bright-eyed, bushy-tailed, powerful girls shrink down to the size of a thimble.

—*O, The Oprah Magazine*, July 2000

As a child, climbing trees was my thing. At the top of an oak tree, I could hear triumphal music, and I could see myself, like Joan of Arc, leading armies up the side of a hill. I was a conqueror. Then when my family moved to Greenwich, Connecticut, I became this itty-bitty little thing. And all I thought about was being too fat and too shy, and the tomboy turned into someone who was trying to figure out how to fit in and look girlish, and it was horrible. So the second part of that first act was about being popular. Being loved. Becoming an actress. Trying to be loved by multitudes if I couldn't be loved by one.

—*O, The Oprah Magazine*, July 2000

I blamed Mother for the growing distance I sensed between her and Dad. She wasn't doing the right things to make him love her. And what it said to me was that unless you were perfect and very careful, it was not safe being a woman.

—*My Life So Far*, 2005

I THOUGHT I had so little value. I didn't pay attention. If I had found out that I earned less, I would have thought well that's just because I'm worth less.

—*Happy Sad Confused* podcast, January 16, 2018

IT WAS MUCH easier for me to organize on behalf of others . . . than it was to look at issues of gender. That would be the hardest to face, because it meant questioning the foundation on which *my* identity as a woman had been built: Women are meant to please. They can rock all the boats there are *out there*, but they must do what's necessary to keep the man happy at home.

—*My Life So Far*, 2005

I HAD SPENT sixty-two years disembodied, as girls and women do when they feel they're not good enough.

—UC Santa Barbara, May 1, 2006

IN MY PUBLIC life, I am a strong, can-do woman. How is it, then, that behind closed doors, in my most intimate relations, I could voluntarily betray myself? The answer is this: If a woman has become disembodied from a lack of self-worth—*I'm not good enough*—or from abuse, she will neglect her own voice of desire and hear only the man's.

—My Life So Far, 2005

PATRIARCHY TAKES AIM at girls' voices, but it takes aim at boys' hearts.

—UC Santa Barbara, May 1, 2006

I THINK IN some ways, even though men still have more power in our society, it's really hard for boys. Because . . . the loss of empathy, the loss of heart happens so young, they think that's just the way it is.

—Huffington Post, March 10, 2014

Men fear that becoming "we" will erase the "I," the sense of self. For most women, our "I" has always been a little porous, whereas our "we" has been our superpower.

—*What Can I Do? My Path from Climate Despair to Action,* 2020

FOR YEARS I never put any of my awards out; some of them I've even lost. Then I married Ted Turner, and the first time I walked into his office, which was the size of a football field, the walls were lined with all of his trophies. And I thought to myself, "well damn it, it's a woman thing," and so I started to display my trophies.

—*The Dissenters with Debra Messing and Mandana Dayani* podcast, October 8, 2020

IF WOMEN CONTROL their bodies, they control their lives, and we still live in a patriarchal society that doesn't want women to control their lives.

—*WhoWhatWear*, January 7, 2020

NEVER UNDERESTIMATE WHAT might be lying dormant beneath the surface of a back-combed blonde wearing false eyelashes.

—*My Life So Far*, 2005

Feminism

IT'S VERY HARD to be an embodied feminist
when you're in inauthentic relationships.

—*4D with Demi Lovato* podcast, June 16, 2021

I DIDN'T UNDERSTAND what [feminism] meant.
What I thought it meant was that you didn't like
men, and I did like men. So, I was not part of
the women's movement at all. I thought it was a
waste of time.

—*Full Release with Samantha Bee* podcast, September
21, 2020

AS WE MOVED through the decade that we spent
together, I became more of a feminist. And
so, my focus was more and more on women's
empowerment. But it's hard to be a complete
feminist if you're in a marriage that doesn't quite
work.

—on her marriage to Ted Turner, *Jane Fonda in Five
Acts*, 2018

I BECAME AN embodied feminist when I was single and saw Eve Ensler perform The Vagina Monologues. While I was laughing, my feminism carried from my head into my DNA. It took a long time, though, because I was brought up with the disease to please.

—*Porter* **magazine, March 2, 2017**

THERE WAS A space between *Barbarella* [1968] and *Monster-In-Law* [2005], where I didn't really pay that much attention to how I looked on purpose, because I thought that to be taken seriously I had to look like I didn't care how I looked. . . . You can look beautiful and still be a feminist.

—*Grazia UK*, **October 5, 2021**

I THINK I started to become a better actress when I became a feminist. And the reason is, that was where I began to understand more why women are the way they are and what are the cultural and social forces that make them the way they are.

—*Charlie Rose*, August 16, 2011

WHAT WE'RE TALKING about, ultimately, through feminism and through an effort to reduce the toxicity in masculinity, is gonna benefit all of us. We all become winners.

—*BUILD Series*, April 9, 2015

I WAS A good girl. Good girls don't talk about money. Good girls aren't ambitious. [Now] I ask and I fight. It's never too late.

—*New York Times*, September 21, 2018

WOMEN ARE THE fastest growing demographic in the world, especially older women. And if we harness our power, we can change the world. And guess what? We need to. And we need to do it soon.

—**TEDTalks, December 17, 2015**

OLDER WOMEN GENERALLY tend to get braver, less afraid of being up front in expressing their anger.

—*Time*, **September 3, 2020**

GENDER INEQUALITY IS so deeply ingrained in our culture that we tend to consider it a fact of life, as something that can be explained away by bogus biology or deterministic arguments. This is the real danger of conservatism—not so much its resistance to change, but its denial of even the possibility of change.

—**National Conference for Media Reform, February 21, 2009**

THE NEWS IS gendered. Would the autobiography of a male actor who had been married to famous women be characterized in quite the same way? For that matter, would my fitness videos have been reported in the same way? Or instead, might they have made me governor of California?

—on the news coverage of her memoir, National Press Club, April 14, 2005

THE OPPOSITE OF patriarchy is not matriarchy; it's democracy.

—National Conference for Media Reform, February 21, 2009

Female

Friendship

IT'S BAKED INTO our DNA, this importance of
gathering together as women. I think it's our
superpower.

—**Greenpeace USA, September 4, 2020**

MOST OF MY women friends are younger than
me, and braver than me, and they challenge me,
and make me better and put starch in my spine.

—*Bazaar UK*, **March 25, 2021**

I HAVE A lot of compassion for men, because
women, no kidding, women's relationships, our
friendships, are full-disclosure. We go deep.
They're revelatory. We risk vulnerability. This is
something men don't do.

—**TEDTalks, December 17, 2015**

I DIDN'T HAVE much parenting, so it's really been
my women friends that have taught me how to
be.

—*New York Times*, **September 2, 2020**

I EXIST BECAUSE I have my women friends.
... They make me stronger. They make me
smarter. They make me braver. They tap me on
the shoulder when I might be in need of course
correcting.

—**TEDTalks, December 17, 2015**

YOU SO OFTEN see women in our media
competing with each other. I like that [*Grace and
Frankie*] is two women befriending each other.
That's very good for people to see.

—*DuJour,* **Spring 2015**

IT WAS JUST so great that I had someone with me
who I could trust. I know she's not going to try to
knife me in the back or steal scenes.

**on working with Lily Tomlin on *Grace and Frankie*,
BUILD Series, April 9, 2015**

I JUST FEEL really lucky because Lily is a true pioneer and she is a genius. Nobody can do what she does.

—*BUILD Series*, January 15, 2018

WE JUST GET along really, really well. I love Lily. We're best friends. . . . We laugh a lot, especially at two in the morning when we've been working for sixteen hours.

—British Film Institute, November 16, 2018

LILY'S FIRST TAKE on everything is humorous. It's why I love to be with her. I try to make some of that rub off on me.

—*Keep It!* podcast, March 25, 2020

WOMEN'S FRIENDSHIPS ARE like a renewable source of power.

—TEDTalks, December 17, 2015

Part VI

ENVIRONMENTALISM

Not a Drill

WE MUST START to live our lives as if this is an emergency, because it is.

—*New York Times*, December 5, 2019

THIS IS THE last possible moment in history when changing course can mean saving lives and species on an unimaginable scale.

—National Press Club, December 17, 2019

I WOULD LIE in bed having conversations in my head with the members of the Senate who deny or delay on climate, feeling impotent because I couldn't find the words that would make them understand what's at stake and persuade them to do something.

—*What Can I Do? My Path from Climate Despair to Action*, 2020

I WAS GOING insane, I was so depressed, knowing things were falling apart and I wasn't doing enough. Once I decided what to do, all that dropped away.

—*The Guardian,* September 5, 2020

INSPIRED BY GRETA [Thunburg], I decided to move to Washington D.C. and hold what we're calling Fire Drill Fridays. You see, Greta said we have to behave like we're in a crisis. We have to behave like our house is on fire, because it is. So, Fire Drill Friday. And every Friday, we have a rally that focuses on a specific topic—oceans, women, war and military, forests, human rights, migration—and how they are affected by climate change.

—*WhoWhatWear,* January 7, 2020

ONE OF THE selfish reasons that I wanted to do Fire Drill Fridays the way we did, which is each Friday we focus on a specific issue, is because I wanted to learn, I wanted to know more.

—Greenpeace USA, September 4, 2020

THE PENTAGON PAPERS were to the Vietnam War what I think the IPCC 2018 report was to the climate crisis: irrefutable proof of lying and deceit on the part of people in power.

—What Can I Do? My Path from Climate Despair to Action, **2020**

VOTING IS UTTERLY critical. We have to vote. I hope that people will understand that we have to vote with the climate in our hearts, with nature in our hearts because we have . . . very little time.

—UnStyled **podcast, February 12, 2020**

IN THE MIDDLE of this crisis, there is no longer a material difference between climate deniers and climate delayers.

—Newsweek, **September 15, 2020**

NEVER TOO EARLY to remember that There Is No Planet B.

—Instagram, April 22, 2020

YES, WE ARE facing a climate crisis. But we're also facing an empathy crisis. An inequality crisis. It isn't only the Earth's life support systems that are unraveling. The fabric of our society is unraveling.

—**National Press Club, December 17, 2019**

THE REALITY, WHICH is not simply a state of consciousness but is based in science, is that we, the species of animal known as homo sapiens, are interdependent with all living things including other animal and plant forms. This is true on the deepest molecular level.

—*Jane Fonda* **blog, July 2, 2020**

THE QUESTION OF why older women are best suited to take the lead in saving the planet: We have the time, the wisdom, the breadth of vision, and the numbers.

—*What Can I Do? My Path from Climate Despair to Action,* **2020**

WE ARE NEVER going to solve climate—or a whole host of related challenges—without women in leadership positions able to decide issues that affect their lives.

—*What Can I Do? My Path from Climate Despair to Action*, 2020

THE CLIMATE MOVEMENT must be a peace movement because to stop wars is to stop the fossil fuel industry and to stop the fossil fuel industry is to stop wars.

—*Jane Fonda* blog, November 9, 2019

OUR CAMPAIGNS NEED to move beyond NIMBY (Not in My Back Yard) to NOPE (Not on Planet Earth) so that when we stop a fossil fuel project or other polluter, it's gone—not just moved.

—*What Can I Do? My Path from Climate Despair to Action*, 2020

WE HAVE TO not waste so much. We have to be satisfied with less. I'm trying to not buy anything new anymore, no new clothing. But I also understand that I can say that because I still wear what I wore 30 years ago, and I have a lot of clothes, so it's easy for me.

—*Interview Magazine*, October 7, 2020

TO BE PREPARED we need to care for each other. Realize that this collective, existential crisis cannot be dealt with individually, or by a small, under-funded, under-staffed government that caters to the fossil fuel industry. We are seeing that the health of the most vulnerable people among us is a determining factor for the health of all of us.

—*Jane Fonda* blog, March 31, 2020

We truly can't address the climate crisis separately from the other issues we face like economic inequality and racism.

—Greenpeace USA, October 23, 2020

IF WE GAIN good policies but hatred and resentment continue to fester in too many Americans, we remain just one bullying, dog-whistling autocratic president away from climate apartheid.

—*What Can I Do? My Path from Climate Despair to Action*, 2020

WE ARE ALL affected by environmental problems one way or another. Those of us with more power and greater influence need to collaborate with those on the front lines, rather than condescendingly "helping others." That's how we build just relationships for just futures. Think solidarity, not savior.

—*What Can I Do? My Path from Climate Despair to Action*, 2020

I'M VERY MUCH attracted to people who don't just talk about the change that's needed, but are willing to put their bodies and lives on the line.

—**Greenpeace USA, December 24, 2020**

WHEN I WAS very young, people didn't fly across the country, they took trains and that's what I did, with my family, or relatives. And let me tell you, when the Green New Deal becomes a reality and we get light rail, electric, fast, I urge you all to take trains. You'll see this beautiful country of ours and fall in love with parts of it you may not have known. And if you fall in love, you'll want to save it.

—*Jane Fonda* blog, May 3, 2021

WE CAN'T STOP making noise until they hear us and act.

—Instagram, June 7, 2021

IF YOU'RE A celebrity, it's your responsibility to use that celebrity, especially when the future of mankind is at stake.

—National Press Club, December 17, 2019

THIS IS NOT the end. But if we start right now,
we can make this the beginning—not of a crisis,
but of a future worth fighting for.

—*Newsweek*, **September 15, 2020**

EACH OF US one day will have to answer this
question: What did I do to protect the planet for
our children, our grandchildren, and so many
precious species while we still had time?

—*New York Times*, **December 5, 2019**

RIGHT NOW WHAT I'm feeling is that I don't
need to motivate them. They're motivating me.
. . . We can't let them shoulder this burden by
themselves, so grannies unite.

—on young people in the climate movement, *Dare I Say*
podcast, May 8, 2020

WHILE IT'S IMPORTANT to write about the tragic impacts of climate crisis, it's also important to give people a hopeful vision of what can be.

—**National Press Club, December 17, 2019**

IT'S TOO LATE for moderation. If the fossil fuel industry hadn't lied to us about what their own scientists told them 30 years ago, if we had acted then, moderate, incremental change might have been enough. No longer. So mobilize, march, rally, vote, act in crisis mode. Hear our youth. That's what I will do.

—**Instagram, September 21, 2019**

I BELIEVE THAT we are lucky to be alive at this time. We are the generation that can ensure there will be a future for humankind. What a glorious responsibility. We must not shirk it.

—***Interview Magazine*, October 7, 2020**

Jail Time

CIVIL DISOBEDIENCE HAS to become the new norm.

—*Time*, September 3, 2020

WHEN YOU SEE how successful [civil disobedience] can be, as long as there are enough people making a ruckus, it's hard not to be hopeful.

—*4D with Demi Lovato* podcast, June 16, 2021

HERE I WAS about to turn eighty-two, and I thought, if I can be arrested every week, I think it will help people engage in civil disobedience. People will realize if this eighty-two-year-old woman is going to do this, maybe it's something I should pay attention to.

—on launching Fire Drill Fridays, *Keep It!* podcast, March 25, 2020

EVEN THOUGH YOU'RE being handcuffed and put in a situation where you have absolutely no control, it's like stepping in to yourself. I have chosen to put myself in this position where I lose all power because of something I believe in. And it's incredible.

—*Elle*, **April 1, 2020**

I'D BEEN WARNED by my lawyer, "If you do it again, then they're gonna put you in jail again." And so, I thought, Well, that's good, because if I turn 82 in jail, that is gonna get a lot of press.

—*Bust Magazine*, **Winter 2021**

As I WAS being led away by the police with my hands in ziplock cuffs, I was filmed shouting, "Thank you. I'm honored!"

—*What Can I Do? My Path from Climate Despair to Action*, **2020**

We don't do civil disobedience as a first effort, but we have been petitioning, writing, marching and begging the government and they don't hear. We've used every lever of democracy and, so, we have to take a step further.

—*The Tonight Show*, January 7, 2020

I KNEW THE jail drill: lots of layers to soften the metal slab.

—*What Can I Do? My Path from Climate Despair to Action,* 2020

THE PLASTIC HANDCUFFS hurt more than the metal ones and I discovered that it's not easy for an 82-year-old to get in and out of a police paddy wagon without the use of her hands.

—*Jane Fonda* blog, October 11, 2019

TED DANSON AND I joined many others to engage in civil disobedience. I caught sight of his face as he was handcuffed. He was radiant.

—*What Can I Do? My Path from Climate Despair to Action,* 2020

IT'S VERY HARD in life to find a way to align your body with your deepest values, and that's what civil disobedience can do.

—*Elle,* April 1, 2020

Part VII

HEALTH & WELL-BEING

Body

I think exercise was for me a healthy way to control my body in a way I couldn't do otherwise.

—*The Guardian,* **September 5, 2020**

The tyranny of perfection forced me to confuse spiritual hunger with physical hunger. This toxic striving for perfection is a female thing. How many men obsess about being perfect? For men, generally, good enough is good enough.

—*My Life So Far,* **2005**

Eating disorders don't represent a lust for food. It represents a loss of authentic self.

—*Huffington Post,* **March 10, 2014**

I was on this toxic quest for perfection, and it is toxic. I should have known better because I saw lots of women who weren't perfect who were beloved.

—*Oprah's Master Class: The Podcast,* **September 19, 2018**

ONE OF THE things about bulimia is that it's
a disease of denial. You know, it takes a lot of
subterfuge. You're very tired, and you're very
angry, and you're very self-hating. And I realized,
I'm heading into a really dark place, and I either
am gonna head to the light or I'm gonna succumb
to the dark, and it's a life or death thing. I went
cold turkey. It was really, really hard. There was
something about taking control of my body,
in that way, that got me over the addiction. It
changed my perception of myself.

—*Jane Fonda in Five Acts*, 2018

AS YOU GET older, with each binge, the fatigue
and the hostility and the self-loathing lasts
longer.

—on why she quit bingeing in her 40s, PeopleTV,
September 20, 2018

WHAT THE WORKOUT did for me was fill in that hole. It made it easy for me to not go back to having eating disorders. It was a way that I could kind of control my body without having to do bad things to it.

—*Decoder Ring* podcast, October 12, 2020

THIS IS A class to warm you up and get you going. Having the correct posture while you do the exercises is very important. Remember to keep your spine long and straight, from your hips all the way up to the top of your head. Pull up tall out of the waist.

—*Start Up with Jane Fonda* workout program, 1987

THERE ARE TWO sides. What got me into it was my move from eating disorders to compulsive exercising. So what's bad about it is that it was compulsive in the beginning. But it is a healthier way to deal with body image than having eating disorders.

—on The Workout, *O, The Oprah Magazine*, July 2000

I CAN'T EVER pretend that I am totally rid of body anxiety. I'm not.

—*I Weigh with Jameela Jamil* **podcast, April 23, 2021**

I ALWAYS TRIED, in the books I wrote, to make it clear: Thin is not the goal. But I was thin. So no matter what I said, the subliminal message was, "You have to look a certain way." And I'm not happy about playing into that.

—**on The Workout,** *O, The Oprah Magazine*, **July 2000**

STARTING WITH *KLUTE,* I began to re-inhabit myself, and my voice began to drop. . . . I went back and looked at all my movies, and I could see my voice, which used to be *way up here*, start to drop as I started to get agency over my life.

—*New Yorker*, **September 26, 2018**

TO KNOW ME is to know that I think exercise is worth it.

—*The Late Show with Stephen Colbert*, **May 1, 2021**

EXERCISING IS AS much about the head as it is about the body—they're not really two separate things. It's very important for mental stability and a good attitude to work out.

—Grazia UK, October 5, 2021

I DIDN'T REALIZE [The Workout] was semi-pornographic actually. When I look at it now I get embarrassed. I could show you now stuff that I'm doing that I'm ashamed of. But it *really* worked.

—Wired, January 22, 2019

I'M HERE TO encourage people that if they can't do what they used to do, it doesn't mean they should do nothing. The key is to do anything—just do it more slowly.

—Los Angeles Times, January 17, 2011

YOUR PHYSICAL CONDITION is not who you are. It does not define you. Don't let it define you. There are so many much more interesting aspects to life, like your heart, your soul, your mind. These things are not affected by your back. Emphasize those kinds of things.

—on staying positive after back surgery, *Mondays with Marlo*, September 21, 2012

IT'S ON PUBLIC record. I couldn't lie if I wanted to.

—on her age, *Charlie Rose*, April 17, 2006

I'M THE BRAND ambassador for L'Oreal for older women, but nobody's ever had a brand ambassador my age. I competed with Margaret Mead, and what they have me doing is hand cream, face cream, and embalming oil.

—*Late Show with David Letterman*, May 19, 2009

I'M GLAD THAT I look good for my age. But I've also had plastic surgery, I'm not gonna lie about that. On one level, I hate the fact that I have had the need to alter myself physically to feel that I'm okay. I wish that I wasn't like that. I love older faces. I love lived-in faces. I love Vanessa Redgrave's face. I wish I was braver. But I am what I am.

—*Jane Fonda in Five Acts*, 2018

I WANTED TO gain a little more time as an actor.

—on getting plastic surgery, *Charlie Rose*, August 16, 2011

I FEEL SO good, I'm so happy, and I didn't want to look kind of tired and jowly anymore.... I like my crow's feet and I like my laugh lines. It was just the little jowls away, that's all.

—*Larry King Live*, April 5, 2010

I THINK IT'S important to live with the awareness of death. Because it makes every moment matter. And instead of running away from it, embrace it. . . . I want to own every moment and be as healthy as I can.

—*Charlie Rose*, **April 17, 2006**

NOW, DON'T GET me wrong. I hate getting old— it's a vanity and joints thing. But I knew that I would have to do what I usually do when I'm scared of something: sidle up to it, get to know it, and make it my friend.

—*My Life So Far*, **2005**

IT'S NOT ABOUT how you look, it's about how you feel. I can do more with ease and grace now at 52 than I could when I was 20. I can ride my bike 60 miles, I can handle stress, I have good muscle tone. That's what it's about. Not about being thin but about being healthy.

—*Washington Post*, **March 13, 1990**

I WORK WITH teens. And then I'm seventy-two and I'm writing a book about Boomers and seniors and the other end of the life span. And they have something in common. When people are fit and healthy and strong, they're empowered. They don't feel helpless. You know, young kids tend to feel powerless. Older people sometimes can feel powerless. When you take charge of your health, it gives you power.

—*Larry King Live*, April 5, 2010

I DIDN'T THINK I'd make it past thirty. I thought I would die of, I don't know, alcohol or drugs and all by myself, all alone. I saw no future.

—*Happy Sad Confused* podcast, January 16, 2018

AT 65, I never thought I'd have a career. And a hit TV show! I'm 80! I keep pinching myself! I can't believe it! I didn't think I would live this long!

—*The Guardian*, May 27, 2018

I THINK IT'S a hoot that, at my age, people are calling me a fashion icon.

—*W Magazine*, May 19, 2015

I SUPPOSE I'VE always known what I like on my body. . . . I'm best when I'm wearing something structured, with no frills or bows. Something that will show my waist and bum, because I've always had a good bum.

—*W Magazine*, May 19, 2015

Mind

THERE IS NO doubt the most important relationship we have is our relationship with ourselves.

—Being a Teen: Everything Teen Girls & Boys Should Know About Relationships, Sex, Love, Health, Identity & More, March 4, 2014

I HAVE COME to believe that when you're actually *inside* oldness, as opposed to anticipating it from the outside, the fear subsides. You discover that you are still yourself, probably even more so.

—Prime Time, 2011

TRYING TO GROW empathy within yourself is revolutionary.

—BUILD Series, April 9, 2015

MY EYESIGHT IS going but my insight is more acute.

—Jane Fonda blog, July 29, 2020

FAME AND CELEBRITY doesn't assuage the pain of loss of self-esteem.

—*Charlie Rose*, **April 7, 2005**

I USED TO walk into a party and think, "Oh, my God, will I be interesting enough? Will people like me? Will I be pretty enough? Do I fit in?" Now I go into a room and think, "Do I really want to be here? Are these people I want to spend a few hours with?" It's a big shift.

—*O, The Oprah Magazine*, **July 2000**

I WAS ASHAMED of myself. I wasn't proud of the life that I was living. So I thought, if I pretend to be generous, maybe eventually I will become generous. If I pretend to have a spine, maybe I will become brave. And you become what you do.

—*WTF with Marc Maron* **podcast, March 28, 2021**

IT'S NOT HAVING experiences that makes us wise. It's reflecting on the experiences that we've had that makes us wise and that helps us become whole.

—**TEDxWomen, December 8, 2011**

DON'T GIVE UP that effort to learn from your wounds and your scars.

—***BUILD Series*, April 9, 2015**

I DIDN'T KNOW what I wanted to do, which is very common today for young people. It's really hard to be young. And I found it very hard, and I floundered around for quite a long time.

—**"Explains It All" from *Harper's BAZAAR*, March 25, 2021**

ASK QUESTIONS. STAY curious. Stay interested. It's much more important to be interested than to be interesting.

—**American Film Institute, June 5, 2014**

I AM ALWAYS studying. I'm a student. I didn't do necessarily well in school, but I always study and become obessive and go deep down into things.

—CUNY TV's *Theater Talk*, May 1, 2009

I THINK AS you get older, you teach what you need to learn.

—Advocates for Youth, September 26, 1997

I ALWAYS FEEL that I've got to pay attention so I can learn. And I try to have friends who can teach me. I'm a student. I'm a generic kind of person. I'm very observant. I receive it. And then I become the megaphone. I don't invent things. You have to know where your strengths are. I'm derivative; I'm not original.

—*Harper's BAZAAR*, March 25, 2021

DEPRESSION IS SORT of like Eeyore; it hangs over me all the time. What I have found is that . . . when I put my body on the line for something that is important to me, the depression lifts.

—*The Dissenters with Debra Messing and Mandana Dayani* **podcast, October 8, 2020**

I DON'T GET bored, and I don't get lonely.

—*Conversations* **podcast, September 11, 2021**

YOU MAY DISCOVER, as I did, that a lot of things that you used to think were your fault, a lot of things you used to think about yourself, really had nothing to do with you.

—**TEDxWomen, December 8, 2011**

I CAN'T PRETEND that it's easy to still your mind; it's not easy. But it's like riding a bike. You can't, you can't, you can't and then you can. You have to just keep doing it. Don't give up; it takes time!

—**on meditation, *Shape Magazine*, December 29, 2014**

NOT ONLY AM I not in a panic about my wrinkles and my age, but not a day goes by that I don't realize you get wiser as you get older. You stop blaming others for patterns you realize are your fault, and you begin to realize "I shouldn't do that because it will lead to this."

—*Washington Post*, October 28, 1977

Spirit

IT TOOK ME a long, long time to realize we are not meant to be perfect. We are meant to be whole.

—*Oprah's Master Class*, January 9, 2012

IT'S THE ACT that I call "beginning." The first one is called "gathering," because I think the first thirty years is when we gather the tools and the scars and the wounds and the resilience and everything else that makes us who we are. And for me, the second act, from thirty to sixty I called "seeking," because that's when I turned my eyes outward.

—on the third act, *Charlie Rose*, April 7, 2005

THIRD ACTS ARE important. It's the way you can kind of make sense of the first two acts of your life, and I wanted to know how I should live the end of my life. And I'm eight years into it now. And I've become a full, whole human being finally.

—*Charlie Rose*, April 17, 2006

I REALIZED THAT I'm not afraid of dying, but I'm afraid of having regrets.

—Bazaar UK, March 25, 2021

I'VE ALWAYS BEEN a big believer in taking leaps of faith. It's my main form of exercise these days, taking big leaps.

—Greenpeace USA, May 28, 2021

WHEN YOU TAKE a leap of faith you don't always land in the right place, but you sure do learn things. It's good for the heart.

—The Guardian, May 27, 2018

I WAS LIKE an empty chalice looking to be filled. I didn't know what I wanted to be filled with. I made a few mistakes about what it was that I was trying to fill myself with. But it was spirit. It was reverence. It was wholeness and completeness, and that's the journey that I'm on now.

—Charlie Rose, April 7, 2005

FOR THOSE OF us who harbor old ghosts (doesn't everybody?), it is in our relationships that they surface, and then we are confronted with a choice: Either we learn to manage the ghosts or we settle for distance or instability.

—My Life So Far, **2005**

I NEVER WANTED to settle for who I was. I didn't like myself and I always wanted to get better and I've been very intentional about that and I think I have gotten better.

—The Times, **September 8, 2020**

EVERYTHING CAME LATE to me: my voice, my becoming whole, my learning intimacy. All those things happened after I turned sixty.

—Oprah's Master Class: The Podcast, **September 19, 2018**

THE LONGER YOU live, the more it's "been there, done that." Well, I've hit bottom and I've survived. So, you separate the wheat from the chaff. You learn not to make mountains out of molehills. It's called wisdom.

—"Explains It All" from *Harper's BAZAAR*, March 25, 2021

POWER HAS TO come from inside. It has to come from knowing who you are, why you're on earth, what is the meaning of your life.

—*Harper's BAZAAR*, March 25, 2021

FEELING THAT I have used my life for good, that I have always tried to be a better person and tried to do good in the world. That's what makes me feel worth it.

—*Grazia UK*, October 5, 2021

I'VE BEEN IN all kinds of situations: I've been shot at, I've had bombs dropped on me; but I tend not to be afraid. Maybe emotional intimacy scares me. That's where my fear lives.

—*The Guardian*, September 5, 2020

I HAVE BEEN brave enough to continually get out of my comfort zone.

—*I Weigh with Jameela Jamil* podcast, April 23, 2021

THERE ARE DAYS when I feel very confident, and there are days when I feel I should pack it in, that I'm a complete fraud, . . . that I could make a long list of people I know who can do everything better than I—and that includes mothering, cooking, acting, producing, working out, everything.

—*Chicago Tribune*, December 29, 1986

I'M A QUINTESSENTIAL late bloomer—but since we're living an entire adult lifetime longer than our parents and grandparents, it's kind of good to be a late bloomer.

—New York Times, **September 21, 2018**

WHEN I START down a path that I know is the right path, I go with all of me.

—The Guardian, **April 04, 2005**

IT WASN'T SO much that I felt sad about all the wasted time, because I wasn't fully authentic, but on the other hand, why not instead just be proud of yourself that you got there and you didn't stop trying?

—The Guardian, **May 27, 2018**

WHEN I MAKE a detour and change, I do it like 500%.

—I Weigh with Jameela Jamil **podcast, April 23, 2021**

I'M HAPPY TO say I am still a work in progress. I have a feeling that the moment before I die I'm going to say, "Oh my God, I get it."

—*The Times*, September 8, 2020

IF I DIDN'T laugh at myself I'd be crying.

—*The Guardian*, September 5, 2020

IT REALLY STRIKES me how little attention I paid early on to how I came across, how I looked, how I was in the world. It is striking. I think if I had been more self-conscious, I would have made fewer mistakes.

—Washington Post, January 7, 2013

YOU CAN'T MAKE your life longer, but you can make it deeper, and the way you make it deeper is by being intentional.

—*Bazaar UK*, March 25, 2021

I WAS SO old at twenty. I was ancient at twenty.
I'm eighty-two now; I am so young.

—*UnStyled* **podcast, February 12, 2020**

I'D LOVE TO be able to do it over again, but never
to go back the way I was.

—on geting a "do over" in life, *Charlie Rose*, **March 11,
2014**

FOR ME THE "good old days" were really the "so
so old days." I spent far too much time worrying
that I wasn't good enough, smart enough, thin
enough, talented enough. I can honestly say that
in terms of feelings of well-being, right now is
the best time of my life. All those enoughnesses
I worried about just don't matter as much
anymore.

—*Prime Time*, 2011

IT WON'T HAPPEN quickly, but your ability to be honest with yourself, your desire to make sense of it all, to learn from your mistakes, will permit you to blossom into life.

—*CBS This Morning*, December 15, 2015

HATE IS A heavy and toxic emotion to carry. It does us no good to lug that baggage around. Evil actions, cruel deeds, are the language of the traumatized. We can and should hate the deeds but feel empathy for the traumatized.

—*Jane Fonda* blog, August 8, 2020

SCARED AS WE all are, if we can allow ourselves to be supple and to get on top of what's put us in our place and understand it—then you can survive—and therein lies strength.

—*Rolling Stone*, March 9, 1978

AGING IS A staircase. The upward ascension
of the human spirit, bringing us into wisdom,
wholeness, and authenticity. Age not at all as
pathology, age as potential.

—**TEDxWomen, December 8, 2011**

PERHAPS THE TASK of the third act is to finish up
the task of finishing ourselves.

—**TEDxWomen, December 8, 2011**

I AM OVER the hill in a chronological sense,
but there is a whole vista out there that I didn't
anticipate. So you can reach the peak and then
you can go down and it can be just as interesting.
It's a good idea not to pay too much attention
to what other people think are the peaks and
valleys.

—*The Hollywood Reporter*, **May 29, 2019**

TAKING RESPONSIBILITY AND forgiving yourself
and others are two of the critical things about
getting old.

>—*Washington Post*, September 20, 2018

No IS A complete sentence.

>—*4D with Demi Lovato* podcast, June 16, 2021

I NEVER WOULD have expected my life to get so
much fuller and, in some ways, more meaningful
as I moved into my 8th decade.

>—*Jane Fonda* blog, December 17, 2019

YOUNG PEOPLE, THEY have this long horizon in
front of them. They don't know what they need
and what they don't need and who they need to
know and what they need to get. And it's very
stressful. When you get older, you know what you
can let go of and you become lighter.

>—*Charlie Rose*, August 16, 2011

I HOPE THAT my legacy is to make people understand the importance of living with intention, and, instead—this is really trite—of being a leaf in the river, kind of floating where the current takes you, being in a boat with oars and steering against the current to where you think you need to go. I have been a leaf in the river for a lot of my life.

—*The Cut*, **September 4, 2018**

I OFTEN WONDER how long I will live. I'm perfectly resigned to death, truly I am, but Gloria Steinem once told me she wants to live at least to 100. When I asked her why, she answered, "I want to see how things turn out." That was about 15 years ago and I didn't share her desire then but now I do. I want to see how things turn out or at least if they're headed in the right direction.

—*Jane Fonda* **blog, July 29, 2020**

AS WE SHAPE our own last third of life, so do we help to transform the experience of age for ourselves, our men, and our children . . . modeling what it means to live an examined life of reflection, compassion, and balance.

—*Prime Time*, 2011

WE ALL WONDER what, if anything, we're going to leave behind. My ability to understand what my life means—to put it in a way that can be meaningful to other people—that's the gift I would leave behind. It's the strangeness of my life that is the most important thing about me, more than any particular part of my work.

—*DuJour*, Spring 2015

TIME EXPANDS WHEN we are paying close attention to life, detail by detail, moment by moment. Perhaps this is another purpose of the Third Act. Assuming we are able and want to reduce the to-ing and fro-ing of youth, we have more time to make time for time.

—*Prime Time*, 2011

To BECOME WHOLE, you reach around and pull all those shadows in and they join your light— you put it all together inside your skin. And you accept that, yes, I'm flawed, but my intentions are good, and I will never be perfect, but I will continue to evolve toward that.

—*Town & Country*, **October 12, 2017**

Milestones

1937

- Jane Seymour Fonda is born to actor Henry Fonda and socialite Frances Ford Seymour on December 21. She is named for the third wife of Henry VIII, Jane Seymour—a distant relation—and is called "Lady Jane" throughout early childhood due to this.

- Jane's childhood and the Fondas' family life is perceived as idyllic by the media, but behind closed doors, both parents have mental health issues. Jane, feeling abandoned, often escapes to the outdoors.

1940

- Jane's brother, Peter, is born on February 23. Like Jane, Peter eventually chooses to follow in his father's footsteps and pursue acting as an adult. He's best known for *Easy Rider*, which he produces, co-writes, and stars in.

1949

- *Harper's Bazaar* does a "family picnic" photoshoot of the Fondas at their residence. Henry, Frances, Jane, Peter, and their half-sister from Frances' first marriage, Frances (or "Pan"), are present. The family looks blissful and perfect, but the photos are heavily staged.

1950

- Frances dies by suicide at the age of forty-two while undergoing psychiatric treatment for bipolar disorder in an upstate New York facility. Jane and Peter are told that she died of a heart attack. Eventually, Jane learns the truth from a magazine article.

- Months later, Henry marries a woman twenty-four years his junior and sends Jane and Peter to boarding school. Due to her mother's suicide and her father's detachment, Jane considers 1950 one of the most formative and difficult years of her life.

1951

- Henry enrolls Jane at Emma Willard School, in Troy, New York.

- While in high school, Jane develops bulimia as a result of Henry's expectations of perfection and the long-term mental health impact of her mother's suicide. She continues to face eating disorders throughout her adult life, finally overcoming bulimia in her forties.

1954

- Henry and Jane act in a fundraising performance of *The Country Girl* at the Omaha Community Playhouse, sparking her interest in the arts. The Omaha Community Playhouse is where Henry originally got his start in the acting world as well.

1955

- Jane enrolls at Vassar College.

1957

- After dropping out of college, Jane moves to Paris for six months to enroll in the art school Académie de la Grande Chaumière and experience the New Wave period of French filmmaking. Roger Vadim, Jane's future husband, is associated with the New Wave—the style (choppier editing, mobile film cameras) is used in some of Vadim and Jane's projects together over a decade later.

1958

- After Henry insists that Jane needs to begin supporting herself financially, he moves the family from the East Coast (and Jane from France) to Santa Monica, California. Jane befriends Lee Strasberg's daughter, Susan, and through her, meets Lee (famous for coaching James Dean, Marilyn Monroe, and Paul Newman). He accepts Jane into his Method Acting class, and Jane joins the NYC Actors Studio. Strasberg tells Jane that she has "real talent," the first individual outside of her family who expresses that sentiment. According to Jane, this is "a turning point" in her life.

- To support herself, Jane takes up modelling. She signs with Eileen Ford's modelling agency and is featured on multiple magazine covers—including *Vogue* in 1959.

1960

- Jane makes her acting debut in the Broadway play *There was a Little Girl*, playing a young, wealthy woman who is sexually abused. The play is a flop and closes after sixteen performances, but Jane receives the New York Drama Critics' Circle award for "the most promising actress of the year for drama" and is nominated for the Best Performance by a Featured Actress in a Play Tony award for her work.

- Her second Broadway role in *Invitation to a March* begins later that same year and is well-received. The play runs for over one hundred performances before it closes.

- She also makes her film debut in *Tall Story*, playing a cheerleader. Robert Redford, one of Jane's later frequent film collaborators, also makes his film debut in an uncredited role. Jane continues to book small to medium-sized film roles, including some filmed entirely in French, over the next few years.

1962

- Jane books a job reading radio commercials, recommending that listeners consider joining the army as the U.S.'s involvement in Vietnam ramps up. She's dubbed "Miss Army Recruiting—1962."

1963

- Roger Vadim approaches Jane about working with him on a film, *La Ronde*. She initially turns down the opportunity, though when she meets Vadim again

174   JANE FONDA IN HER OWN WORDS

later that year at her birthday party, they hit it off. Half a year later, and after striking up a romantic relationship with Vadim, she takes on the role in *La Ronde* she initially turned down. Jane continues travelling between France, New York, and California for work.

1965

- *Cat Ballou*, a comedy Western, premieres. Jane is cast as a schoolteacher-turned-outlaw, and stars opposite Lee Marvin. Marvin wins an Academy Award for his performance, and though Jane isn't nominated for any major awards, the film marks a turning point in her career, as it converts her from a young up-and-comer to a bankable star.

- Jane marries Vadim. They live together on an estate in the country outside of Paris, where Jane finds herself catering to socialite gatherings, taking care of her husband's children from his previous marriages, conforming to strict gender roles, and fielding Vadim's requests to bring other women into their bed.

1967

- While filming on location in Baton Rouge, Louisiana, Jane comes face to face with the racial disparities found in the South and across the U.S.

1968

- *Barbarella*, a science fiction spoof and cult hit directed by Vadim, debuts with Jane as the titular character. This film establishes her as an international sex symbol, though Jane later admits that she was so uncomfortable filming certain scenes that she needed to drink copious amounts of alcohol on set to loosen up. While filming this and another film with Vadim, Jane's awareness of the sexual exploitation of women increases.

- Jane watches newsreel clips from Chicago's riots during the 1968 Democratic National Convention, the events made famous by the trial of the Chicago Seven. This sparks conversations with some French actor/activists in Jane's social sphere, which kickstarts her interest in activism.

- Vanessa Vadim, Jane's daughter, is born on September 28. After a difficult birth, Jane experiences postpartum depression for some time. Jane's relationship with Vanessa remains strained throughout Vanessa's childhood and early adulthood and only improves later in both of their lives.

1969

- Jane is nominated for her first Academy Award for *They Shoot Horses, Don't They?* This is Jane's first major film that seats her in a "meaty" role, instead of a role that plays into the "girl next door" or "sex symbol" archetypes—Jane dives into the role with the method acting techniques she'd learned at The Actors Studio, embracing her character's grit, spirit, and darkness by living at the studio, detaching herself from her husband and newborn daughter, and sinking into a deep depression. The director, Sydney Pollack, acknowledges Jane's seriousness about acting and asks for her opinion on the script and her scenes—this is the first time she's afforded an opportunity to help make decisions and give input about the film she's in.

1970

- Jane moves back to the United States, taking up residence in her father's house, and begins her life as an activist in earnest. Her interests are wide—she supports the Native American movements to preserve their land and hosts Black Panther fundraisers—but her main focus is ending the war in Vietnam. Her activism takes her from one corner of the U.S. to the other and broadens her perspective about the diversity of the American people.

- Jane is arrested at the airport after returning from an anti-war event in Canada on suspicion of drug trafficking. Only vitamins are found after her luggage is searched. According to Jane, the arresting officer tells her that orders for her arrest came from the Nixon White House—Jane raises a fist in a sign of resistance for her mugshot.

1971

- Alongside actor Donald Sutherland and a number of activist friends, Jane forms the FTA ("Free the Army" or "Fuck the Army") Show, a satirical anti-war, pro-soldier road show that travels to military bases across the U.S. and Asia. Their intention with the FTA Show is to open an honest dialogue with soldiers about their deployments to Vietnam, and is designed to combat sexist, racist war propaganda seen in Bob Hope's USO tour.

- Between the FTA Show and her ongoing anti-war messaging, Jane is placed on the Nixon administration's "enemies list." The FBI begins putting together a file on her.

- *Klute* premieres. Jane is cast as Bree, a sex worker. Originally uncomfortable in a role so outside her realm of experience, Jane shadows New York City sex workers to understand that world in more depth. After diving into Bree's psyche, and realizing they are not so different after all, she agrees to stay on in the role. Jane wins her first Academy Award, a Golden Globe, and a number of other awards for her performance.

1972

- Jane travels to Vietnam on a two-week trip after receiving an invitation from the Vietnamese Committee for Solidarity with the American People. While there, Jane meets with Vietnamese citizens and U.S. POWs, makes radio broadcasts about the situation caused by the war, and documents the destruction U.S. bombs had caused to hospitals, towns, and dike systems. She is photographed on a Vietnamese anti-aircraft gun, resulting in the inauspicious moniker of "Hanoi Jane."

- After returning from Hanoi, Jane deals with the repercussions of her actions, perceived by some as anti-United States and anti-soldier rather than anti-war. Her radio broadcasts get backlash, but the photo of her on the anti-aircraft gun sparks true outrage. Her speaking engagements are protested by right-wing demonstrators or canceled outright. She isn't cast in major Hollywood pictures and is even accused of treason.

- *F.T.A.*, a documentary about the FTA Show, is released within days of Jane's return from Hanoi. It's pulled from circulation in less than a week, and most copies of the film are destroyed. *F.T.A.*'s director speculates that the erasure of the film from the public eye is due to government intervention—that the government paid off the film's distributor because they didn't want the public to see the film's content.

- Activist Tom Hayden (of Chicago Seven fame) partners with Jane to found the Indochina Peace Campaign, an anti-war group advocating for an end to the Vietnam War. Their work kicks off with a multi-city speaking tour, where Jane and Tom aim to begin a grassroots movement to elect anti-war leadership and draw attention to the human rights violations occurring in Vietnam.

1973

- After a period of separation following Jane's decision to leave France and return to the U.S. to join the anti–Vietnam War political movement, Jane divorces Vadim.

- Jane marries anti-war activist Tom Hayden three days after obtaining her legal divorce from Vadim. Their relationship is focused, almost entirely, on

activism and social justice, as Tom finds Jane's acting
career to be "a bit shallow."

- Troy O'Donovan Garity, Jane's son, is born on July 7.
Jane and Tom do not want their son to be burdened
with baggage-laden names like "Fonda" or "Hayden,"
so they instead name their child for two historic rev-
olutionaries, Nguyen Van Troi and Jeremiah O'Donovan Rossa, with the surname of Tom's mother. Jane's
relationship with her son is less strained than her
relationship with her daughter—she and Tom bring
newborn Troy with them on their various adventures,
whereas she and Vadim typically left Vanessa home
with a nanny.

- After receiving a copy of the FBI's file on her and
learning that the U.S. government is tailing her, Jane
sues top U.S. government officials, claiming civil
rights violations. The case drags on for many years,
but in the end, the government admits wrongdoing
and promises to follow more stringent surveillance
guidelines.

1974

- Jane, accompanied by Tom and Troy, returns to Vietnam to film *Introduction to the Enemy*, a documentary
meant to humanize the everyday person in Vietnam
and show the impact the war had and is still having on
them. *Introduction to the Enemy* is the first movie that
Jane produces under her own production company,
IPC Films.

1976

- Tom and Jane found the Campaign for Economic Democracy, a California-based group created to promote leftist ideas like rent control, investment in clean energy, labor rights, women's rights, and anti-war sentiment in government.

1977

- Tom and Jane purchase a 160-acre plot of land near Santa Barbara, California called Laurel Springs and convert it into a performing arts summer camp. Laurel Springs invites campers of all socio-economic and racial backgrounds to attend and uses performing arts to foster community and increase self-esteem. The summer camp stays open through 1991.

1978

- After announcing that she'll only take on film roles that focus on important issues, Jane is cast in and wins an Academy Award for her role as a military wife and VA hospital volunteer in *Coming Home*. The film's focus is the trauma experienced by Vietnam War veterans.

1979

- *The China Syndrome*, an IPC film, is released. Jane stars as an intrepid and persistent reporter uncovering the truth of a nuclear power plant's coverup operation. The nuclear power industry immediately vilifies the film, calling it "character assassination."

The Three Mile Island nuclear accident occurs less than two weeks later, instantly rocketing the film to the forefront of national conversation.

- Jane opens an aerobic exercise workout studio in Beverly Hills. The classes are extremely successful, both because aerobics are accessible to many people and because Jane sometimes teaches the classes—especially the ones early in the morning—herself.

1980

- Dolly Parton and Lily Tomlin star alongside Jane in *9 to 5*, a film about women in the workplace. As an IPC Films-produced picture, Jane has creative control. The film was originally planned as a realistic drama, but after realizing she wants Tomlin and Parton to participate, she reworks the film into a comedy. Parton's song "Nine to Five" is nominated for numerous awards, and the film is nationally recognized as a huge success.

1981

- Through IPC Films, Jane acquires the screen rights for *On Golden Pond*, a play that depicts the fraught relationship between an aging father and adult daughter and parallels Jane and Henry's real-life relationship. She and her father star in the screen adaptation, both earning Academy Award nominations (the film is nominated for ten overall), BAFTA nominations (the film is nominated for six overall), and Golden Globe nominations (also six nominations overall). Henry Fonda wins the Oscar for best actor, but due to illness,

Jane accepts the award on his behalf. Henry dies five months later at the age of seventy-seven.

- *Jane Fonda's Workout Book* is published and becomes a bestseller. Further workout books will follow in quick succession, including *Jane Fonda's Workout Book for Pregnancy, Birth and Recovery* in 1982 and *Women Coming of Age* in 1984.

1982

- A *9 to 5* spinoff TV series premieres on ABC. Though none of the original actors return to their roles for the TV show, Jane is an executive producer for the first two seasons.

- Jane informally adopts Mary "Lulu" Williams. Lulu, the youngest daughter of two Black Panthers, meets Jane as a camper at Laurel Springs Children's Camp, but is adopted into Jane's family after her parents and older siblings are unable to continue taking care of her.

- *Jane Fonda's Workout*, Jane's first workout video, is released and eventually becomes the highest-selling VHS of all time. Jane goes on to make over twenty more workout videos over a span of thirteen years, selling approximately seventeen million copies. Profits from these workout videos are used to fund the Campaign for Economic Democracy.

1984

- Jane wins a Primetime Emmy for her portrayal of an Appalachian wood carver in the made-for-TV film *The Dollmaker*.

1990

- After a year and a half of separation, Jane divorces Tom after he admits that he's fallen in love with another woman. Media mogul Ted Turner calls as soon as her separation becomes public information, asking Jane on a date.

- Jane stars in *Stanley & Iris* opposite Robert DeNiro. It is her last film prior to a fifteen-year hiatus from Hollywood.

1991

- Jane marries Ted Turner. She retires from acting to spend time with Ted on his various properties and uses her time away from Hollywood to rekindle her childhood love and respect for nature. She also explores philanthropic endeavors alongside Ted. Among other projects, she works to increase performing arts exposure to youth in the Atlanta, Georgia area.

1994

- The United Nations Population Fund, the United Nations' sexual and reproductive health agency, declares Jane a Goodwill Ambassador.

1995

- Jane founds the Georgia Campaign for Adolescent Power & Potential (originally the Georgia Campaign for Adolescent Pregnancy Prevention). It begins as a teen pregnancy prevention organization, but the programs offered eventually focus more broadly:

on empowerment, education, and overall health for teenagers.

1999

- Malcom Vadim, Vanessa's first child and Jane's first grandchild, is born on May 28. Malcom's birth kick-starts Jane and Vanessa's push to mend their broken mother/daughter relationship.

2000

- Vadim, Jane's first husband, dies on February 11 at the age of 72. Jane attends his funeral, as do three of his other ex-wives.

- Jane establishes the Jane Fonda Center for Adolescent Reproductive Health at Emory University in Atlanta, Georgia. The foundation aims to prevent adolescent and teen pregnancy by advancing scientific research and distributing information and training to at-risk groups.

2001

- Ted and Jane get a divorce after Jane realizes that she follows similar unhealthy patterns in all three of her marriages—she sacrifices her voice and her sense of self to please her partner. During this period of self-reflection, she finds faith—though Jane considers herself Christian, she doesn't participate in organized religion as much as she focuses on spirituality and something larger than oneself. Jane often refers to Ted as her "favorite ex-husband."

2002

- Jane visits Israel and the West Bank in partnership with V-Day, a nonprofit that distributes funds to grassroots groups working to end violence against women. There, she meets Jerusalem-based groups protesting violence against women and Israel's occupation of the Gaza Strip. She spends her sixty-fifth birthday visiting refugee camps and hospitals.

- Viva Vadim, Vanessa's second child and Jane's second grandchild, is born on November 23.

2004

- Again in partnership with V-Day, Jane helps coordinate the first ever all-transgender production of *The Vagina Monologues*. The event's proceeds benefit the Gay and Lesbian Task Force and the Los Angeles Commission on Assaults against Women.

2005

- Jane returns to acting in the film *Monster-in-Law*, starring Jennifer Lopez. This is one of the few moments in her career that she plans, as she knows audiences will go to the movie to see Lopez but will come out introduced (or re-introduced) to Jane Fonda.

- Alongside journalist Gloria Steinem and poet Robin Morgan, Jane founds the Women's Media Center, a nonprofit that advocates for increasing representation and visibility of women and girls in media, and for diversifying the individuals involved in media so that the stories told about women and girls are more true-to-life. The center creates advocacy campaigns, provides leadership training, and distributes awards to execute their goals.

- *My Life So Far*, Jane's autobiography, is published. The book separates her life into a series of three thirty-year periods, or "acts," and emphasizes that her third and last act will be the most important. It also offers insight into the many contradictions and complexities of Jane's life.

2007

- Jane participates in an anti–Iraq War rally at the National Mall in Washington, D.C. Though she is vehemently against the war, she takes a step back from the vocal role she had during the Vietnam War and instead chooses to elevate other voices.

- The Cannes Film Festival awards Jane an honorary Palme d'Or to honor her extensive and prodigious body of work. She is the fourth person ever to be given this award.

2008

- Jane is inducted into the California Hall of Fame.

2009

- Jane begins blogging, originally intending to use the blog to document her return to Broadway. Her scope quickly broadens to topics like exercise, social justice, and updates on her personal life.

- After a forty-five-year hiatus from the stage, Jane returns to Broadway for the play *33 Variations*. She plays a musicologist battling ALS while trying to discover why Beethoven composed so many iterations of a simple music theme and earns a Tony Award nomination for her work.

2010

- Jane undergoes a lumpectomy after a breast cancer diagnosis.

2011

- Jane's new book, *Prime Time: Love, Health, Sex, Fitness, Friendship, Spirit—Making the Most of All of Your Life* is published. The book gives perspective on aging in a healthy fashion, using anecdotes from her and her friends' lives.

- New *Jane Fonda's Workout* tapes are developed, with a focus on exercises for seniors. Five of the most popular original *Workout* programs are re-released alongside the new senior-focused videos in digital and DVD formats a few years later.

2012

- Jane guest stars as a media company CEO in HBO's *The Newsroom*. The recurring role marks her new interest in television and eventually earns her two Emmy nominations.

2013

- Mary "Lulu" Williams publishes *The Lost Daughter: A Memoir,* a book about her upbringing and adoption by Fonda. In the memoir, Lulu attests that Jane saved her—a wonderful mother figure who helped with homework, listened to her anxieties and fears, and celebrated her achievements, but who also happened to be one of the biggest names in the United States.

2014

- Jane's guide, *Being a Teen: Everything Teen Girls & Boys Should Know About Relationships, Sex, Love, Health, Identity & More,* is published. The book endeavors to give teenagers answers to any and all questions they may have as they get older.

2015

- *Grace and Frankie* debuts on Netflix. The series stars Jane alongside her lifelong friend Lily Tomlin and addresses topics like friendship and romance through the lens of older age—subjects rarely discussed in Hollywood.

2016

- Jane undergoes a mastectomy procedure. When talking about the procedure, she quips that she once was a "sun worshipper" and also needs to go to the dermatologist every time she has a day off.

- The Human Rights Campaign releases a tribute video for the victims of the Pulse nightclub shooting in

Orlando. Jane tells the story of one of the victims and urges viewers to support legislation that protects the LGBTQ community and increases gun control.

- Tom, Jane's second husband, dies on October 23 at the age of seventy-six. Jane, Troy, and Tom's widow, Barbara, put together a memorial to commemorate the impact Tom had on activism, democracy, and their lives.

2018

- *Jane Fonda in Five Acts,* an HBO documentary about Jane's life, premieres. The documentary separates Jane's life into five acts: the first four named after the most influential man in her life at the time (Henry, Vadim, Tom, and Ted), and the last named after Jane herself.

2019

- Jane appears on the cover of British *Vogue* alongside fourteen other influential women like Greta Thunberg, Laverne Cox, and Jameela Jamil, having been selected by guest editor Meghan, Duchess of Sussex. Her first *Vogue* cover was sixty years previous, in 1959.

- Jane is inducted into the National Women's Hall of Fame.

- Peter, Jane's brother, dies on August 16 at the age of seventy-nine. Jane spends a lot of time with Peter before his death and says he "went out laughing."

- Answering Greta Thunberg's call to treat global climate change as an emergency, Jane moves to Washington, D.C. and launches Fire Drill Fridays. The protests on Capitol Hill feature speakers on different aspects of environmentalism—its effects on women, the economy, race, etc.—and call for Congress to pass the Green New Deal. Jane makes headlines as she is arrested four Fridays in a row while participating in civil disobedience.

2020

- Jane's climate change treatise, *What Can I Do?: My Path from Climate Despair to Action*, is published. It features interviews with climate scientists, discusses concerns regarding converting to a climate-friendly future, and outlines Jane's own journey in activism.

2021

- At the Golden Globes, Jane receives the Cecil B. DeMille Award—an honorary Golden Globe given to a single individual every year for "outstanding contributions to the world of entertainment."

2022

- *Grace and Frankie*'s seventh and final season airs. Dolly Parton guest stars, marking a *9 to 5* reunion forty years in the making.

Acknowledgments

We would like to thank Samantha Alvarado, Caitlin Costello, Carr Harkrader, Ji Kim, Grace Lemon, Marga Medina, Erin Rosenberg, Suzanne Sonnier, and Sherry Welch for their invaluable contributions to the preparation of this manuscript.